# Re-energise
# your sex life

# 52 brilliantideas

one good idea can change your life...

# Re-energise your sex life

## Put the zing back into your lovemaking

Elisabeth Wilson

First published in 2005 by
**The Infinite Ideas Company Limited**
Belsyre Court
57 Woodstock Road
Oxford
OX2 6HJ
United Kingdom
www.infideas.com

CIP catalogue records for this book are available from the British Library and the US Library of Congress.

ISBN 1-904902-09-X

Brand and product names are trademarks or registered trademarks of their respective owners.

Designed and typeset by Baseline Arts Ltd, Oxford
Printed and bound by TJ International, Cornwall

# Brilliant ideas

**Brilliant features** ...................................................................................xii

**Introduction** .........................................................................................xiii

1.  **Stop having sex**...........................................................................1
    Bored with sex? Then take a break.

2.  **Getting it right**............................................................................5
    How do you get your lover to love you the way you want to be loved?

3.  **Lust – it's all in your mind** .......................................................9
    Not as interested as you used to be? The easiest way out of a rut is to get sex on
    the brain – literally.

4.  **The least you need to do...**.......................................................13
    ...to keep your relationship minty fresh.

5.  **Join the 30%** ..............................................................................17
    That's the percentage of women who can come purely through penetrative sex. Hmmm.

6.  **Make it a quick one** ...................................................................21
    Do it right and a quickie can deliver the sort of thrills you haven't experienced since
    adolescence.

7. **Say it loud, say it proud – the art of talking dirty** .................................25
I know. You can only bring yourself to talk dirty when you're drunk. Very drunk. So drunk that next morning you can't remember what you said. That's why you need this idea.

8. **Sleep is the new sex – honest!** ...............................29
I know a woman who tried to convince her lover that the really happening people were giving up sex in favour of sleep. But he wasn't buying it and neither am I!

9. **Get over yourself** ...................................35
If bungee jumping could do for us what sex can, we'd be queuing up to try it.

10. **Getting jiggy with your G-spot** ...............................41
Think of the G-spot like Cliff Richard's sex appeal. It might not do much for you, but that doesn't mean it doesn't exist.

11. **Paying for it** ...................................47
Slut sex can be a turn-on for both of you.

12. **The love's there, but the lust's gone AWOL** ...........................51
Hey sexual pioneer! Yes, we're talking to you.

13. **Coming over all touchy-feely** ...............................55
Learn to express sensuality with your whole body.

14. **Surprise!** ...................................59
Isn't it time you got in touch with your creative side?

15. **Something for the weekend** ...............................65
Time spent away together intensifies your experiences. Making sex the focus of your break will revitalise your love life.

16. **Think kink** ...................................................................69

Remember: we don't always get what we want. But we can ask.

17. **Learn the art of kaizen** ................................................73

Kaizen is a Japanese concept that means, 'Small changes, big differences.' It can revolutionise your love life.

18. **Building bridges** ...........................................................77

How can a woman come just like a man?

19. **When your sex drives are out of sync** .........................81

Looking for a mate? Choose someone with roughly the same sex drive. Oh, sorry, you thought you had.

20. **What's your LQ score?** ...................................................85

Imagine you're in the Mastermind chair and your specialist subject is your lover. What would be your love quotient (LQ) score?

21. **Bringing up the rear** .....................................................89

Sorry, terrible pun, but the alternative was 'bottoms up', so think yourself lucky.

22. **Sexual confidence** .........................................................95

What is sexual confidence? And how do you get your hands on some?

23. **What you see...** ..............................................................99

The general consensus is that men get turned on more than women by visual stimulation. But is it true?

24. **Blow jobs 101** ..............................................................103

Put a little thought into your next blow job – he'll appreciate it.

25. **Dressing up and staying in**.....................................................................107
Acting out fantasies takes a bit of practice, but can certainly brighten up a boring Saturday night.

26. **Handy work**................................................................................................113
What they never taught you at art class...

27. **Heading south** .........................................................................................117
Enjoy the journey and she'll be ecstatic.

28. **Short cuts to better orgasms** .............................................................121
We're coming over all PC

29. **Easy routes to faster orgasm for her**................................................125
Quicker, harder, faster? How to come more easily.

30. **Assume the position...**.........................................................................129
...but ring the changes

31. **Bunty and Daisy rather than Sadie and Maisie**................................133
Or for those of you who prefer acronyms – soft-core B&D (bondage and discipline) rather than hard-core S&M (sadism and masochism).

32. **Heading even further south**................................................................139
Few things in life will earn you so much gratitude for a moderate amount of effort as giving great head.

33. **More on blow jobs** ................................................................................145
Can you ever know too much?

34. **The love bath**................................................................149
If you're wise, the bathroom is the place to go to get dirty. Nowhere else in your
house will make you feel so spa-cial. (Sorry.)

35. **Fight club**......................................................................153
Sexual energy isn't the only flow of energy between a long-standing couple.
There's blind fury, too.

36. **The joy of shopping** .....................................................159
Who knew that going to the shops could be so good for your love life?

37. **Play away**......................................................................163
It's safe to say that about ten seconds after some bright cave dweller discovered that the
carrot was good to eat, another one worked out that it was good for something else, too.

38. **Danger**...........................................................................167
Danger is the fastest-acting aphrodisiac.

39. **'Let a woman be a woman and a man be a man'** ...............171
There's a bloke in the States called David Deida who has some interesting ideas as to
why sex goes off the boil.

40. **Tantric sex**.....................................................................175
Not just a load of old joss sticks.

41. **In out, in out** .................................................................179
Breathing. You do it every single minute of your life. Boy, have you been taking it for
granted.

42. **Dirty little secrets**.................................................183
Why every couple needs some.

43. **Just say 'no'**.................................................187
There's saying 'no' and there's saying 'no' nicely. Two very different things.

44. **It's not all in your mind**.................................................191
If you've gone off sex, it may be time to see your doctor.

45. **Pressure – it's not a dirty word**.................................................195
Or rather, if you're doing it right, it can be.

46. **Wait. We said wait!**.................................................199
Delay orgasm – a.k.a. 'peaking' – and you'll know the true meaning of 'climb every mountain'.

47. **Developing sexual mystique**.................................................203
Yes, it's possible. Even if you've shared a bathroom for years.

48. **See things differently**.................................................209
Give yourself a real eye-opener.

49. **Dealing with burnout**.................................................213
That's what we call it when you don't want sex and you just don't care. In fact, you don't seem to care about anything much at all.

50. **Dream time**.................................................217
Sexual fantasy – a short cut to great sex.

51. **Fantasy destinations** ........................................................................223
   Great places to have sex – and you don't have to get a babysitter.

52. **Are you sexually mature?** ...............................................................227
   It is big and it is clever.

**The End** ................................................................................................232
Or is it a new beginning?

**Where it's at** .......................................................................................234
Index

# Brilliant features

**Each chapter of this book is designed to provide you with an inspirational idea that you can read quickly and put into practice straight away.**

Throughout you'll find four features that will help you to get right to the heart of the idea:

- *Try another idea* If this idea looks like a life-changer then there's no time to lose. *Try another idea* will point you straight to a related tip to expand and enhance the first.

- *Here's an idea for you* Give it a go – right here, right now – and get an idea of how well you're doing so far.

- *Defining ideas* Words of wisdom from masters and mistresses of the art, plus some interesting hangers-on.

- *How did it go?* If at first you do succeed try to hide your amazement. If, on the other hand, you don't this is where you'll find a Q and A that highlights common problems and how to get over them.

# Introduction

**We promised you no crummy line drawings of silly positions, no step-by-step instructions on starting your own bisexual swinging club and no illustrations of beardie-weirdie blokes looking masterful.**

We've kept those promises. You'll have read everything in this book before and we don't pretend otherwise. In fact, we're proud of that. Because the success of a book promising to transform your sex life doesn't lie in it's risqué content or indeed (and I'm thinking specifically here about beardie-weirdie guys) its lack of it. A sex book will only work if it's do–able. Readers should want to act on the suggestions rather than just read them for vicarious thrills or, more likely, in growing consternation.

This is a book of sex solutions, not potential problems. So there's nothing in here about safe sex. If you're young, free and single, desperate to mingle and push your sexual boundaries then this book is not for you. Carry on with the group sex in tents at Glastonbury, people. Britain salutes you, but we've been there, done that and we'd rather stay beneath our duvets. This book is for couples who simply want to have better sex with the person they're with. And they've probably been with that person for quite a long time.

What these people want (and I include myself here) are quick, reliable and above all easy ways to reignite the fire. We don't want this to involve expensive props, embarrassing encounters, bri-nylon nurse's outfits or to interfere with our soap opera habit. And that's where this book comes into its own. I decided to write it because I believe that the 52-ideas format is the best possible way to encourage people not simply to read but to experience. Because of my work, I've read more sex books than most other people have had orgasms and I know that for sex advice to work you have to actually act upon it rather than simply read it. So, all of the ideas have been tested by real couples (thanks, and I promise not to reveal your names). The very simplest ideas can have you feeling new sensations or rediscovering old favourites, as I found out after undertaking my very first piece of 'research' involving nothing more than a bottle of vodka (see IDEA 24). As we all know, but tend to forget, the basis of great sex long-term is that old chestnut, communication. And I discovered that it doesn't take a lot to get you talking to each other again about what you like and what you don't. At the very least, these ideas can give you a great laugh when they go wrong and can blow your socks off when they go right.

Sex in most long-term relationships isn't the most important component, but my own feeling is that if more of us were to give it a much higher priority we'd be a lot happier. To quote Erica Jong, 'There are things that happen in the dark between two people that make everything that happens in the light all right.' For very little effort, you can improve your sex life greatly. It says 52 ideas on the cover of this book but in my pernickety way, I've counted them and there are actually 403. If you and your partner try just ten of these over the next twelve months (much less ten weeks), you'll improve your love life beyond recognition. This is more than you can say about line drawings of the 'split bamboo' position.

# 1

# Stop having sex

**Bored with sex? Then take a break.**

*Focusing on sensuality rather than sex can remind you why sex is worth bothering with in the first place.*

The top tool in the sexual counselling box of tricks is a technique called 'sensate focus'. To put it baldly, you make a pact not to have penetrative sex. When couples go to see a sex therapist, they will often be asked to refrain until they've worked through their 'issues'. Couples will often spend weeks simply holding each other, working up to touching each other non-sexually through techniques such as massage and then finally moving on to sexual pleasuring without penetrative sex. If you got stuck at the beginning of the last sentence, focusing on the word 'weeks' with a sort of sick dread, then relax. You don't have to give up sex for all that long to get astounding results.

Giving up sex completely sounds extreme, but couples find that taking a holiday from disappointed expectations and performance pressure – instead spending time getting to know each other again through strictly non-penetrative contact – works wonders when they want to regain their passion. Ripping apart old patterns of

Here's an idea for you... **Don't focus on the outcome. Don't consciously try to arouse your partner. Concentrate only on touch. The person being touched should try to dissolve into it and concentrate on the sensations. This is a sort of meditation for both of you and should at the very least help you to relax when you're frazzled.**

relating to each other means couples get back to basics. Simply spending time with each other trying to make your partner feel good is powerful. You'll remember what all the fuss was about in the first place.

Sex expert Tracey Cox says sex is like chocolate – if we get too much of a good thing we go off it. Think how much better chocolate tastes after you've given it up for Lent. It's the same thing with sex. Too much and we get jaded and take it for granted.

You might be far from needing sex therapy, but there are very few couples who wouldn't benefit from a spot of sensate focus. It encourages better communication and sparks libido.

Choose a week when you both decide that you won't have penetrative sex.

**Day 1**   On the first night you cuddle up together on the couch.

**Day 2**   Go to bed an hour early. Naked. Lie in bed stroking and touching each other. Talk about your lives. Reconnect.

**Day 3**   Take a shower or bath together with sensual oils.

**Day 4**  She gives him a long all-over massage.

**Day 5**  He gives her a long all-over massage.

**Day 6**  She massages him, including touching him sexually but not to the point where he has an orgasm. She can explore his reactions to various kinds of touching and ask for feedback.

**Day 7**  He does the same for her.

**Day 8**  By now the sexual tension between you should be causing visible sparks!

**Try sensate focus in your bathroom to give a whole new meaning to good, clean fun. Look at IDEA 34, *The love bath*.**

*Try another idea...*

**'He was the kind of guy who could kiss you behind your ear and make you feel like you'd just had kinky sex.'**
JULIA ALVAREZ, American writer

*Defining idea...*

3

How was
it for
you?

**Q** **We don't have a clear week to devote to this. Any ideas?**

A   *Try some speed sensate focus. Like speed dating, but less embarrassing. Use a spot of sensory deprivation to help you focus on the power of touch. It's a brilliant reminder when we're tired and wired that our bodies can give us supreme physical pleasure. The more senses that are cut off, the more we appreciate the ones that are left. Blindfold your partner and then insist they relax totally for the next fifteen minutes. They could wear earplugs, too, to really sink into their own world of sensory delight. Play some soft music for your benefit and light some candles. Ask your partner to lie back on comfortable pillows or a duvet. They should be naked and you should either be lightly dressed or naked. The room should be warm! Using a long feather or a soft silk scarf, stroke every part of your partner's body, not just the usual erogenous zones. Keep the touch gentle and continuous. Finally, blow gently over their skin everywhere the feather or silk touched. You can then swap over.*

**Q** **What if I'm just not comfortable with all that touchy-feely stuff?**

A   *Ignore your need for sensuality – and that of your partner's – at your peril. The need to be held lovingly is fundamental to humans. Scientists believe it could be as important in our behavioural development as food and water. We crave sensual touch and for many of us sex is the means whereby we get it. Orgasm could simply be the payoff that nature's built into our physiological make-up to make sure we seek out physical closeness, especially where women are concerned since orgasm isn't strictly necessary for reproduction.*

# 2

# Getting it right

**How do you get your lover to love you the way you want to be loved?**

Just because you've been together forever, doesn't mean you press each other's buttons absolutely perfectly. Yet the man or woman who can tell their lover that they want to be touched differently from the way they've been touched a million times before is pretty rare.

There are ways to ask without embarrassing yourself and mortifying your lover. Here's how to get your lover to do something differently when they think they've been getting it right for years.

Here's an idea for you... **Always find something positive to say, but don't praise what's bad. Pretending to enjoy what you don't enjoy is what's got you in this mess in the first place!**

## THE WRONG WAY

Using phrases starting with 'Why don't you...', 'You never...' or 'That doesn't...' will cause offence and your partner will get defensive. Moreover, whining is deeply unattractive.

## THE RIGHT WAY

### Step 1: Praise, praise, praise – your new resolution

From now on, you're going to be an appreciative lover. You're going to praise your lover's performance every chance you get and using every way you can think of. This will create a 'win–win' situation. Be especially appreciative during sex. Do it with body language. Do it loudly. Spell it out: 'I love everything you do in bed', 'You're just so sexy', 'No one's ever done that to me the way that you do'. They should finish every session assured that you're blissfully happy.

If you're not an appreciative lover, make this your *modus operandi* from now on. For one thing, this technique will backfire spectacularly on you if it stops as soon as you get what you want – it will look like a cynical ploy. (That's because it *will* be a cynical ploy.) So wise up, there's nothing to be ashamed of in creating confidence in your lover. Their 'win' is that you're creating an atmosphere where they can't fail. They won't fear trying something different if they don't feel that your happiness is dependent on it. If they get it wrong or if they don't want to go through with it, they've nothing to lose because they know just how much you value them. Your 'win' is that besides being a lovely person you're also gearing them up for moving your sex life on to greater heights.

## Step 2: Focus on the positive

Once you've created a climate of confidence, you can modify their technique by focusing on the positive. For instance, 'I love the way you do that, especially when you go slowly/quickly/hang off the bedside table while you're doing it.' The other great bonus of this approach is that within reason it doesn't matter if it's a complete lie. For example, your lover may fellate you with the speed of a rotodriver, but if you tell her how lovely it is when her mouth goes really slowly she'll probably believe you. She'll almost certainly start doing it slowly too. The payoff for you is that you'll get more of what you want.

This clearly can be overdone. She's obviously going to get suspicious if she never hangs off the edge of the bedside table while doing it yet you can't stop talking it up. Use discretion and be specific if possible. And you really need to use your hands to gently direct the action the way you want it.

## Step 3: Suggest how they could change

Now you can suggest doing it differently. This has to be done with grace and it has to be done lightly, not as if your entire sexual happiness depends on it (remember they can't fail). Say that you've read about something you'd like to try in a book and ask if they would oblige....

See **IDEA 17**, *Learn the art of kaizen*, **and get more of what you want.**

*Try another idea…*

'The secret to telling someone they're the worst lover you've ever had, is…not to. Focus on what you want, not what you don't…Start by focusing on yourself, not your partner's [faults]. Make a list of ten things you want more of in bed, ten things you want less of, and ten new things you'd like to try. You have to know what you want in bed in order to get it.'
TRACEY COX, *Supersex*

*Defining idea…*

7

How was it for you?

**Q** **Tried this but my lover is very self-conscious. Any other ideas?**

**A** *Some couples find it helps to use the virgin fantasy when they're trying something new. Another version is the alien fantasy. Basically, one of you is a virgin/alien and has no idea what sex is. The other person has to explain what they should do, how they should behave and what they should say. This works well because the shyer, more self-conscious person isn't in control – they're only following instructions.*

**Q** **His oral sex technique has improved a lot, but it's still not hitting the right buttons. What now?**

**A** *If your communication is good then you're just going to have to show him. Make it during a very steamy session where you're both a bit crazed with passion and he wants to do anything to get you off. Ask him, 'Would you mind trying this? I've been thinking it would really drive me crazy.' Then show him with your own tongue, on his bicep, palm or any other flat surface (men can do this on a woman's finger or toes) – make sure he can see what your tongue is doing and how fast it's going. Back this up with instructions, but only a little at a time. Aim for a 10% improvement every time. And praise, praise, praise.*

# 3
# Lust – it's all in your mind

**Not as interested as you used to be? The easiest way out of a rut is to get sex on the brain – literally.**

Researching this book has thrown up some surprises for me and one of them has been the effect on my own libido.

Always an 'average' on the sex-o-meter – in other words, I'm not the girl most likely to suggest a love-in with the neighbours – thinking, reading and talking about sex for three months has had an extraordinary effect on my sexual response. I don't mean that I've been tempted to give swinging a try, but having sex on the brain has definitely increased my desire for sex and I'll now advise people that the simplest way to ensure you have (and want) more sex is to *think* about it more regularly.

As time goes on, we become subsumed in the minutiae of our lives – the fetching, carrying, hunting, gathering. But as sex writer Ann Hooper says, 'You can try every sex position you can think of, including dangling from the ceiling, but if you don't bring your fertile brain into play, you may not manage to become aroused.'

The secret is to fantasise. But first you'll have to rethink your idea of what sexual fantasy means.

**Read sexy romance novels or soft porn. Listen to music that makes you feel sexual – whatever it is, if it rocks your boat, play it loud and play it often.**

*When did you consistently have the best sex you've ever had?* Most of us would say in the first few months of getting it on with a new partner, hopefully the partner we're still with. Why? New love of course, or new lust at the very least. The principal reason that the sex at the beginning of a relationship is so outstanding is that it's fantasy-fuelled. New lovers spend just about every minute they're not in bed with their lover fantasising about their lover. Their minds are constantly running over what they got up to the night before and what they'd like to be doing next time they meet. They walk around in a fug of erotic fantasy. And this fuels their sexual encounters. The second they see their lover they're primed and ready to go.

We tend to think it's the person that fuels our desperation for sex, but physiologically it's got just as much to do with the mind being constantly focused on doing the deed and the signals this sends to our body. So, if you've wistfully looked back on the way you used to feel about each other and if you firmly believe that you can't reconstruct that lust, try thinking about sex more. Any thoughts you have – no matter how fleeting – count. Think about sex during the day, and when the chance to have sex turns up you're far more likely to be enthusiastic. Just a touch will get the juices flowing. On the other hand, if nary a sexual thought has fluttered across your mind during the day, your lover is going to have an uphill and probably futile struggle to get you to even try.

**Count the number of people you meet in a day who actively appeal to you. Seek to get aroused by other people, but obviously don't act on it. That old chestnut about taking the energy back to stoke the home fires isn't an old chestnut for nothing.**

Counsellor Sarah Litvinoff says, 'Sex therapists often find that women who claim never to have been sexually interested or who have gone off sex, never think sexual thoughts. Many people narrowly define sexual fantasies as the mini-pornographic scenes you play out in your head, which might include, say, bondage or lesbian images, that are a mental turn-on, but which you wouldn't necessarily enjoy enacting for real. But, in fact, *any* sexual thought is sexual fantasy.' And any sort of sexual thought gets the job done.

Turn to IDEA 50, *Dream time*, for more on the power of the mind.

Try another idea...

Let your mind wander, look for the lascivious and feel the throb of sex that is lying beneath the layers of our sophisticated lifestyle. Find stimulation in your daily routine and you'll find yourself overspilling with erotic charge, which will translate into action. You will initiate sex and respond to your partner in a different way sexually. You'll be gagging for it.

Begin to make a habit of daydreaming about sex. First thing when you wake up in the morning or last thing before you go to sleep, think a dirty thought or two. When you're commuting, let the last time you made love run through your mind. As you're queuing or waiting for your train, relive your sexual greatest hits. Remember that every time sex flits across your mind it's a fantasy, and that those who fantasise most have the best sex lives.

**'You are what you dream. You are what you daydream. Masters and Johnson's charts and numbers and flashing lights and plastic pricks tell us everything about sex and nothing about it. Because sex is all in the head.'**
ERICA JONG

Defining idea...

NB Like faith healing, you don't have to believe in this for it to work.

How was it for you?

**Q** **I feel a bit mean fantasising about anyone but my wife. What can I do?**

A    *One woman I know visualises herself slamming any averagely attractive man she meets against the wall and kissing him wildly. On the surface she's shaking hands and mouthing platitudes. The men know nothing of it, but the sexual frisson created by those images fuels her own idea of her sexual self. Her reasons for doing it have absolutely nothing to do with a desire for infidelity. She says, 'It's like being teenager again. When anyone remotely attractive came into your sights, no matter how "unsuitable", you'd start flirting and wondering about a possible liaison, obviously not going anywhere because you were fifteen. Fantasising like this keeps me young.' It's harmless, it's cheap, it's private. But there's no law that says you can't fantasise about your partner in this way if you want. Next time you see a cute waitress, imagine it's your missus bringing you a latte in that low-cut top instead.*

**Q** **I don't have a sexual thought in my head that vaguely interests me. Where can I begin?**

A    *OK, start this way. Imagine yourself being as sexually attractive as you can be. In your mind, you're drop dead gorgeous. Move onto visualising this gorgeous you having sex. Stick with this for a while and see what happens.*

# 4

# The least you need to do...

**...to keep your relationship minty fresh.**

Read, digest and ponder. Then get your diary, a big red pen and start prioritising your relationship.

This chapter contains the three golden rules of a healthy relationship – the *sine qua non* of sexual happiness. All the technique and creativity in the world isn't going to fix the sex in a relationship where the couple is together but not *together*. On the other hand, couples that spend time together, and anticipate and plan for those times, find it hard to lose interest in one another.

## RULE 1: DAILY...

How is your partner feeling right now? What's happening at work? How are their relationships with friends, colleagues, siblings, parents? Carve out fifteen minutes of every day to talk. If you find yourselves getting into a rut of busy-ness, when you pass like ships in the night for several days in a row without touching base, either go to bed before your usual time or get up earlier and have a coffee together so you can touch base.

*Here's an idea for you...* **Look for easy ways to cheer your partner up. Pick up a tub of her favourite ice-cream on the way home from work. Run him a bath and bring him a beer. Sappy gestures work – they build up a huge bank of goodwill that couples can draw on when life gets stressful.**

Kiss each other every morning before you get out of bed. Take the time for a swift cuddle. Breathe deeply. Hold tight. Do the same at night. Never take your physical intimacy for granted. In this Vale of Tears we call life, you found each other. Pretty amazing. Worth acknowledging that with at least a daily hug, methinks.

### RULE 2: WEEKLY...

Go out with each other once a week where humanly possible. Once a fortnight is the bare minimum. According to the experts, this is the most important thing you can do. Couples who keep dating, keep mating. Spending too long sloping around the same house does something to a couple's sexual interest in each other and what it does generally isn't good. So get out, preferably after making some small effort to tart yourself up so you're visually pleasing to your partner. Let them see why they bothered with you in the first place. (No, I never said this chapter was rocket science. I just said that it worked.)

### RULE 3: MONTHLY...

*Try another idea...* **The appointment system in IDEA 8, *Sleep is the new sex – honest!*, is a good option if sex has turned into a rushed afterthought.**

Go for a mini-adventure – shared memories cement your relationship. Make your adventure as mad or staid as you like, but at the least make sure it's something that you haven't done since the beginning of your relationship. It really doesn't matter what it is, as long as it's not your usual 'date'.

What's the point? You see your partner coping with new environments and new skills and that keeps you interested in them. And them in you. Simple.

*'Good sex begins when your clothes are still on.'*
MASTERS and JOHNSON, sex research pioneers

*Defining idea...*

If you're shaking your head and tutting 'how banal', I'd get that smug look off your face, pronto. Research shows quite clearly that one of the defining differences between strong couples and 'drifting' couples is the amount of effort and time they spend on their shared pursuits. All of us have heard the advice, 'Spend more time with each other being as interesting as possible.' But how many couples do you know who actually do it? I'm prepared to bet that those who do seem happiest.

**Q   How do you expect us to get out once a week?**

*How was it for you?*

A    *You don't have to go out for long – an hour or two is fine. Even parents of newborns can find a way if sufficiently motivated.*
*No money? Make it a challenge to have a good night out on a tenner or less. If all else fails, go for a walk and treat yourself to half a pint of lager at your local. Oh OK, share half a pint if money's really tight.*
*No childcare? Make it your mission to seek out other couples with kids who live locally – ideally, in the next street – and look like they enjoy going out (single parents and confirmed stay-at-homes are no good for this). The deal is that one half of their couple comes to your house and sits with your kids once a week. The next week one of you returns the favour. It means that for one night's babysitting you get two nights out and an evening home alone. Not bad.*
*No conversation? You'd better fix this one before you do anything else.*

15

**Q** **We couldn't come up with anything we wanted to do for a mini-adventure. Any suggestions?**

*A*    *Here's a year's worth:*

- *hill walking between two cosy pubs*
- *hiring some cycles*
- *al fresco dining, with champagne and strawberries*
- *horse riding*
- *paragliding*
- *spending a weekend in a city you've never visited before*
- *punting along a river or taking out a rowing boat in your local park*
- *watching a matinée at the cinema*
- *spending a day at a health spa*
- *visiting an art gallery*
- *going to the theatre*
- *attending a self-help seminar*

*Take turns to suggest the adventure, and go along with your partner's choice even if you don't fancy it. Even the disasters will give you shared memories to laugh about afterwards.*

# 5

# Join the 30%

**That's the percentage of women who can come purely through penetrative sex. Hmmm.**

I think 30% is putting it too high. I reckon it's nearer to 10%. Other surveys report that around 90% of women have orgasms only through oral sex or masturbation, and that sounds much closer to the truth.

My point being – most women don't come through penetrative sex. Those of you ladies who do, there's still a big debate over what's rocking your boat. It could be indirect stimulation of the clitoris or rhythmic rubbing of the anterior vaginal wall (home of the elusive G-spot). Anyway, enough about you already.

This chapter is primarily aimed at the majority of women who haven't yet come from straightforward sexual intercourse. There are various ways of making this happen. There are lots of ideas bridging techniques and the G-spot, but here is the low-down on the one position that's designed to give constant clitoral stimulation during genital intercourse: the coital alignment technique (CAT). A useful one to master because, let's face it, constant clitoral stimulation is no doubt going to up

Here's an idea for you...

**Women: once you've got the hang of the rocking movement squeeze your pelvic and thigh muscles as often as you can remember. This again increases friction and pressure on his penis. Good for you. Good for him. Result!**

your chances of having an orgasm during sex. So much so that the man who first brought the CAT to our attention in the early 90s, Edward Eichel, got a bit carried away and trumpeted it as the only guaranteed way to achieve simultaneous orgasm during sex.

Well, from experience and from anecdotal evidence I'd have to disagree. The CAT doesn't always deliver. According to Eichel's studies, however, 77% of females achieve orgasm 'always or often' this way and 36% of couples had simultaneous orgasms. Whatever, greater clitoral stimulation plus the judicial use of other techniques as needed has to mean that more women achieve more orgasms during intercourse. A good thing.

Ironically for the position that delivers the porn-star ideal – orgasm from penile penetration – the CAT is a great big girl's blouse of a position. In a perverse way, I kind of like the idea that it's almost impossible to do while getting down and dirty.

**What you can expect?** Slow (very slow), gentle and tender sex; a subtle dance between lovers.

**What you can't expect?** Absolutely no deep, hard or fast thrusting or shouting of 'Give it to me good, big boy.' You'd actually feel a bit stupid shouting that during the CAT. It's more of a 'I really love you' – 'No, I really love you' – 'Not as much as I love you' position. You get the picture.

If you and your lover are at the stage of intimacy (preliminary) where you can only have loud, dirty and fast sex (oh, stop showing off) then the CAT is probably not worth bothering with. But if you're the sort of couple that cares enough to read this – in other words, you share a lot of intimacy and a lot of lurve, sometimes too much – then you'll be happy with the opportunity for lots of eye

**Turn to IDEA 30, *Assume the position*, for more on positions that improve stimulation for both partners.**

*Try another idea...*

contact and prepared to give it the time it takes. You'll need it. Women: don't even think of giving this a go if you're still pissed off with him for dodging out of the washing up.

## SO GET ON BOARD

After assuming the missionary position, the man should move up the woman's body a few inches. His pelvis should be aligned with her vulva, directly over it. This means that only the tip of his penis is 'in'. This also means (and this is the whole point) that the greater part of his penis is pressing up against her vulva, pressing on her clitoris. Forget thrusting, think friction.

His legs should be together and straight; her legs should be wrapped around his thighs, with her ankles resting on his calves so her legs are as straight as possible. This means she will be opening her vagina and labia, again increasing friction. As a true gentleman, his weight should be taken on his elbows, but now he should put his arms under her armpits and let himself rest gingerly on her.

*'I blame my mother for my poor sex life. All she told me was, "The man goes on top and the woman underneath." For three years my husband and I slept on bunk beds.'*
JOAN RIVERS

*Defining idea...*

Now for the difficult bit (you think I'm joking?). What you want to do is rock. No thrusting. She should tip her pelvis away from him down into the bed so his penis comes almost all the way out and then he should push down so he moves lower down her body and enters her fully. She tilts up to meet him, pulls her pelvis down so that he comes out again and he pushes down with his pelvis so he moves back into her again. Her clitoris should be feeling constant pressure at all times. Carry on, and on, and on. Don' t think of achieving orgasm, just get into the rhythmic dance. Don't thrust. Don't rush to orgasm. Slow and steady, that's the ticket. It's not easy, but when you get the rhythm it will all fall into place and feel natural. It helps if she sets the pace.

*How was it for you?*

**Q    Tried the CAT. She came first. How can we guarantee simultaneous orgasm through intercourse alone?**

A    *You can't. Nothing can. Keep practising.*

**Q    It felt good, but it took aeons. Any refinements you could suggest?**

A    *No time for the full-blown CAT? You can try what I call the 'half-CAT'. After assuming the missionary position she should close her legs so both feet are together with him still inside her. He should place his legs on either side of hers. This doesn't give the same clitoral stimulation as the CAT, but it does increase the pressure on the clitoris. The downside is that he'll fall out if he thrusts too hard. Another alternative is for the woman to get on top. She takes him inside her and then closes her legs, as he opens his. Be careful now. She scoots up his body so she maximises clitoral stimulation and then carry on as per.*

# 6
# Make it a quick one

**Do it right and a quickie can deliver the sort of thrills you haven't experienced since adolescence.**

Many couples applaud the quickie — it fits nicely into their schedules. But it isn't really a 'quickie' if it happens in bed. That's just a snatched shag. For the same amount of time or effort you could take your sex life to another level.

The essence of the quickie is surreptitiousness, not speed. The reason the quickie needs to be fast is not that you're supposed to be doing something else instead, like making Sunday dinner for the in-laws, but that at any moment your mother-in-law could pop her head round the kitchen door and offer to help with the gravy. Until you've had a quickie where there's every chance you could get caught in the flagrant act, you haven't really had a quickie at all.

Here's an idea for you...

**Women: initiating a quickie is a way to stay close to your partner during times when he's distant and you're busy. Women on the whole are pretty rubbish at making men feel desired. We expect their never-ending sexual interest in us but don't reciprocate. There's nothing like initiating a quickie to make him feel desirable. It's the equivalent of him buying you a dozen roses.**

Doubt the aphrodisiac qualities of being caught? Think of all the couples you know who have maintained chronically dysfunctional but illicit 'relationships' for years – convinced they're in the grip of a great passion. The truth is that they wouldn't have lasted five minutes if their sex life wasn't almost entirely sneaky and speedy. Quickies make for addictive sex.

Now some people don't like quickies. They really don't. They might have gone along with it when you first got together because frankly they'd have had sex suspended from Big Ben if you seemed to think it was a good idea. But it's not really them and they don't feel comfortable if they think they'll get caught. They can't bear the thought of being embarrassed (usually men). They don't like getting messed up (usually women). And they don't even get an orgasm out of it (almost certainly women). So if your lover's in this category, you have to accept 'no' gracefully or keep on trying but be prepared for a lot of rejection. Alternatively, you could just get very good at persuading your partner that fast, hot sex up against a wall is the best idea they never had.

**IMAGINE...**

Any minute now you're expecting some guests to arrive. You're checking the barbie's hot enough or that you've got enough gin, when you catch sight of your partner passing by looking gorgeous. You reach for them, throw them against a wall, ravish them with kisses, hands roaming over and under clothes. Your lover is surprised, but begins to kiss you back passionately. You both go from 0 to 70 in seconds. You glance at your watch. Your guests are expected to arrive in precisely five minutes. No time to undress. At any moment you could hear a ring on the doorbell. You fumble, push underwear aside, undo zips and buttons, reveal skin, pull clothes up and down so you achieve penetration. Fast and frantic sex is the only kind you've got time for. By the time your guests arrive, only a slight breathlessness gives away your secret.

**Still not convinced? Read more about the aphrodisiac power of the element of surprise in IDEA 14, *Surprise!***

*Try another idea...*

## ANY PROPS?

None. Except if you're a woman with a predilection for quickies it helps if you choose easily accessible knickers. There's something delicious about pushing aside the fabric and it adds to the erotic charge. Thongs are good, but the bloke can end up with friction burns. French knickers? Oh yes.

## GOOD POSITION?

Standing up is the traditional 'knee trembler', but this isn't terrific for any woman weighing more than eight stone. It's even worse for her man. However, you don't have to go for the full monty. Instead of him taking the whole weight of your body, the woman can use a chair or table to support one leg. Or better still, he enters her from behind with her bent over slightly, so he has a good view of his penis entering. Grabbing her as she's going up the stairs and throwing her down on them gives you both a bit of support, although it can be heavy on the carpet burns.

*'I love the lines men use. "Please, I'll only put it in for a minute." What am I? A microwave?'*
BEVERLY MICKINS, American comedian

*Defining idea...*

*How was it for you?*

**Q**   **I'm not very good with the idea of getting caught. It doesn't excite me; it makes me feel sick. Any suggestions?**

*A*   *Try the half-quickie. Its seductive power has nothing to do with getting caught but in making your partner feel that there's nothing in life you'd rather do than have sex with them. You just can't wait another minute! And that's a huge turn-on for anyone. The perfect scenario is when you're preparing to go out, ideally to a social event that's more important to you than your partner. Harass them about being punctual. Emphasise the importance of getting there with loads of time to spare. Get ready just a little bit earlier yourself so they feel slightly wrong-footed by your extreme punctuality. As you're hassling them out the front door, pause as if you've just remembered something and then, looking them straight in the eye, grab them and whisper, 'Well, I guess they can wait another ten minutes.' They should be delighted. If babysitters are involved then you'll have to be more adventurous. Garden shed? Car? Round the corner from the restaurant where you're meeting friends? Live a little. Just make sure you won't be surprised.*

**Q**   **I've initiated quickies twice and they've both been disasters. My partner was totally uninterested. What should I do next?**

*A*   *Ditch the getting caught element totally and instead concentrate on persuading your lover to have sex with you spontaneously in a place you wouldn't normally do it. If they don't go for that, they might just not like the whole idea. But you must discuss it. Why is your partner uninterested? Can they give good reasons that you understand? If you find it hard to discuss this, work on your communication with each other.*

# 7

# Say it loud, say it proud – the art of talking dirty

**I know. You can only bring yourself to talk dirty when you're drunk. Very drunk. So drunk that next morning you can't remember what you said. That's why you need this idea.**

The right combination of pure filth whispered into your lover's ear at the right moment will catapult them into a thundering orgasm. But get it wrong, and they'll be running for the door.

Done right, a few lewd and lascivious words is the simplest way of making your sex life sing – no props or cost involved. If your shagging style has been silent of late, don't suddenly unleash your potty-mouth persona without some warning otherwise your partner will be perplexed at best, turned off at worst. As writer Brigid McConville points out in her book *Our Secret Lives*, there's a big taboo about talking about sex in our culture. Couples who start off filthy, don't stay that way. She says, 'The Big Ban on sex talk can start almost immediately in a relationship, intensifying to solid silence as the years go by. And by the time you've clocked up ten, twenty or more years, it's a hard habit to break.' Quite. So take it gently.

*Here's an idea for you...*

Talk dirty with conviction. Commit to your talk. Talking dirty comes easily when you're in the first few stages of lust, purely because talking dirty is easier with strangers. But when you've shared countless school meetings, and fights over the remote, it's a lot harder. The other side of this is that you must try extra hard to support your lover's efforts. Don't undermine them with inopportune sniggering.

## FOUR WAYS TO ADD VALUE TO YOUR VERBAL

### 1 Give feedback

The most basic form of dirty talk is to describe what's happening to you and what it feels like. For example, 'I love it when you kiss my collar bone like that.' Or 'It's such a turn-on watching your breasts from this angle.' Giving a running commentary on what you're feeling and appreciating also serves to keep you 'in the moment' making it less likely you'll start wondering who's going to get that promotion at work or if you have enough milk for breakfast. So encourage, praise, comment.

### 2 Build anticipation, make them beg

Tell your lover what you're going to do to them just before you do it. Ask them if they like it. Ask them if they don't. Ask them to ask nicely for what they want. Ask them to ask not so nicely. You get the idea. Before you know it, they're talking dirty, too. (However, use this tactic with discretion. Endless questioning can swiftly move from the sublime to the downright annoying, risking the passion-melting retort 'Will you bloody well get on with it!')

### 3 Role-play makes it easier – a lot easier – to talk dirty

Think how much easier it could be if you were pretending to be someone else...

### 4  Read bedtime stories to each other

It's not inhibition that gets in the way sometimes – it's lack of inspiration. After another hard day at the coalface that's contemporary 21st-century life, making up a dirty scenario is just too much like hard work. That's when it pays to have a porn mag kicking about under the bed. Women are often turned on by stories geared towards men and soft porn will supply most couples with some inspiration for reading aloud.

But if that's too 'right-off' for you, *Forum* magazine and the *Erotic Review* are aimed at both sexes and available at a newsagent near you. Or you could try reading a chapter a night from a Black Lace novel, which are aimed at exciting women but will also do the job for men. Another classic for reading to each other is *My Secret Garden*, a collection of women's sexual fantasies by Nancy Friday.

### FINAL WORD

Nobody can give you a script for talking dirty. Transcribed, it always sounds ridiculous. You need to develop your own style together. The main thing is to just do it. Once you start saying dirty words out loud – even if they're someone else's dirty words – you'll soon find your groove.

*For explosive orgasms, combine what you read here with IDEA 28, Short cuts to better orgasms.*

Try another idea…

*'If they call it "dick", don't call it "hot, throbbing cock", if they call it "yoni", don't call it "gaping axe wound". (In fact, don't ever call it that.) If in doubt use the basic anatomical name. You can get more creative later.'*
EM and LO, sex agony aunts on nerve.com

Defining idea…

*How was it for you?*

**Q** **I can't pluck up the courage to talk dirty. I'd like to, but I doubt if my boyfriend would go for it, as he doesn't even talk. How can I do this without looking ridiculous?**

A   *The quiet lover isn't uncommon. If your partner is of the silent school of lovemaking then you may never get them to mutter filth in your ear. But you can try. First, concentrate on getting any noise out of them. Groan, moan and whisper endearments while you come yourself and ask them to do the same for you. Tell them that a little non-verbal feedback will encourage your performance. After groans, work together on eliciting a few words. 'Yes' and 'please' are a start, and if you've been with a silent lover that will seem like a Shakespearean monologue!*

**Q** **What if your partner talking dirty turns you off? Mine says things that make me feel a bit sick, especially when he starts talking in a sort of baby talk and referring to my breasts as 'titties'.**

A   *It sounds as if he's either uncomfortable with talking dirty or thinks he's really good at it. If he's uncomfortable, you need to talk to him directly and find out if this is really turning him on or just his way of seeming willing. Tragically, it might be the second option: he thinks he's a wizard. Always be wary of those people who think they're really good at talking dirty. Inevitably, they're a little bit embarrassing, even if you love them. You need to retrain him, but you need to do it subtly. However, you shouldn't put up with that 'titties' thing for a moment longer. We all have our personal pain threshold and he's stamping all over yours. Next time, look him in the eye, lower your voice an octave and purr seductively, 'Darling, I like to hear them called breasts.' That should do it.*

# 8

# Sleep is the new sex – honest!

**I know a woman who tried to convince her lover that the really happening people were giving up sex in favour of sleep. But he wasn't buying it and neither am I!**

You'd like to have more sex, really you would. You're just too darn tired. Competitive tiredness between couples is a relatively new phenomenon and one result of both partners being strung out with exhaustion is no nookie.

Couples frazzled by the sheer weight of the goals they set themselves compete as to how tired they are. You've worked for it and by god you've got it – a life so totally, overwhelmingly busy that you simply don't have the energy for sex.

It's not of course the end of a relationship if you go some time with a lacklustre or indeed non-existent love life. Every relationship has its down-time. But the major worry with the tiredness reason for avoiding sex is that it gains a weird sort of reverse momentum. Keep using tiredness as an excuse and before you know it, total inertia has set in. What you need is a two-pronged attack.

*Here's an idea for you...* **If sex usually takes place just before bed and is generally rushed and unsatisfying because you're both knackered, make a weekly tryst for sex where you go to bed early and enjoy each other. Therapists agree that this 'appointment system' is one of the easiest ways to ease you back into a good sex life.**

## FIRST PRONG – GET OVER YOURSELF

Here's a fact: having sex when you're tired is not against the Geneva Convention. Having sex when you're tired can start off indifferently and get a whole lot better. And even if it doesn't, I'm firmly of the camp that believes that in a longstanding relationship, indifferent sex is better than no sex. At least you've got something to work on.

If you're of the aficionado brigade who unless sex is a multiorgasmic garden of delight would rather not bother, then you have to negotiate this with your partner. Make definite dates when you're going to do it. Make sex that day your priority. See it as a red-letter event.

## SECOND PRONG – REORGANISE YOUR WORKLOAD

This is anecdotal, based purely on my experience of knowing a lot of couples in their thirties with young children and having no sex. At the root of it is usually resentment on the part of one partner towards the other. Usually the woman is resentful of the man. She is usually working, even if only part time, and doing most of the childcare too. Women who have given up work to look after their children tend not to be as resentful, but they feel that their men don't appreciate all that they do. This is my experience but it's backed up by at least two recent surveys.

*Try another idea...* **Read IDEA 44, *It's not all in your mind* – there may be medical reasons for your tiredness.**

## WHO DOES THE MOST AFTER A
## HARD DAY'S WORK?

This quiz gives couples a quick visual reference of who does more around the home. Tick the sex of the partner who most often undertakes a particular task. This test can be an eye-opener for couples that think they have a pretty equal relationship. If it's not so equal, you have to take steps to delegate or equalise your workload, or your sex life is unlikely to get back to normal any time soon.

*'He said, "I can't remember when we last had sex." And I said, "Well, I can and that's why we ain't doing it."'*
ROSEANNE BARR

*Defining idea...*

| | | |
|---|---|---|
| Getting the children ready for the day | M ☐ | F ☐ |
| Making breakfast | M ☐ | F ☐ |
| Making packed lunches | M ☐ | F ☐ |
| School run | M ☐ | F ☐ |
| Supervising homework | M ☐ | F ☐ |
| Teacher's meetings | M ☐ | F ☐ |
| Immunisations, trips to GP | M ☐ | F ☐ |
| Dealing with childcare | M ☐ | F ☐ |
| Bathing children and getting them ready for bed | M ☐ | F ☐ |
| Bedtime stories | M ☐ | F ☐ |
| Arranging play dates with other parents | M ☐ | F ☐ |
| Supermarket shopping | M ☐ | F ☐ |
| Cooking evening dinner | M ☐ | F ☐ |
| Clearing house at end of evening | M ☐ | F ☐ |
| Paying bills | M ☐ | F ☐ |
| DIY, organising repairs | M ☐ | F ☐ |
| Cleaning | M ☐ | F ☐ |

| | | |
|---|---|---|
| Taking out rubbish | M ☐ | F ☐ |
| Buying children's clothes | M ☐ | F ☐ |
| Washing and drying clothes | M ☐ | F ☐ |
| Dishwasher loading | M ☐ | F ☐ |
| Gardening | M ☐ | F ☐ |
| Maintaining and cleaning car | M ☐ | F ☐ |
| Organising social life | M ☐ | F ☐ |

You might be reading this and thinking, 'I'm the major breadwinner, I work my butt off and can't do childcare too.' But you'll have to find some compromise for the sake of your relationship. You need to talk openly about how you divide your joint workload, give each other the space to have a life as an individual and find time to spend as a couple. If you're reading this and thinking, 'Who needs a blinking quiz to tell me I do it all?' Then stop and examine your martyr-syndrome. Yes, you've got one. At all costs, you have to get rid of it or 'I'm just so tired' will sound the death knell for your sex life.

Overprotective parents take note: someone else can very well look after your children. Your relationship with one another can't be tended by anyone else but the two of you.

Workaholics take note: pop your clogs tomorrow and someone else will fill your job/role/career by Monday morning. No one else can take your place in your relationship.

**Q** **Your advice to make a date for sex just felt like another thing to add to my to-do list. Isn't this approach a bit, well, functional?**

*How was it for you?*

**A** *Yes, I can see why you'd think that. And it's not that I'm unsympathetic, but my point is that you can't rely on spontaneity and lust to propel you into sex. My advice to you is the same as to women who are pregnant and don't fancy sex. Indeed, it's the only advice I give to pregnant women (who ask!): stop relying on your hormones; start relying on your bloke. Relaxing and giving your partner the chance to get you in the mood can often work wonders. Promise yourself that you'll let him do his darnedest to haul you from lethargy and you'll be amazed how often it actually works and you feel your libido stirring. If, after ten minutes or so of foreplay, he still can't persuade you that sex is more worthwhile than sleep, too bad, you'll just have to break it to him gently that tonight he's flying solo. Nine times out of ten, however, you'll have sex.*

**Q** **We have small kids and both work full time. We barely see each other, much less make love. Any fire-lighting tips?**

**A** *The best piece of advice I ever received on keeping the home fires burning was from a sophisticated woman in her forties. She had a grown-up family and a gorgeous husband who was devoted to her after twenty-five years of marriage despite (to my certain knowledge) a host of young women's desperate attempts to seduce him. When I asked her how they kept interested in each other after so long she told me, 'Well darling, we always make a point of going to bed at the same time as each other – early, around ten. [Significant pause] And I always get into bed naked.' Try it.*

# 9

# Get over yourself

**If bungee jumping could do for us what sex can, we'd be queuing up to try it.**

There are minor and major reasons for periods when we don't fancy sex much. Sometimes we simply can't be arsed.

Answer 'yes' or 'no' to these questions:

1. Do you enjoy sex when you get going and then think, 'We should do this more often'?
2. Are there any physical reasons you avoid sex?
3. Are there any psychological reasons you avoid sex?
4. Do you simply prefer to read gardening catalogues or watch *Big Brother* than have sex?

If you answered 'yes' to questions 2 and 3, then this idea isn't going to help. If you answered 'yes' to 1 and 4 then it's time for some tough love. You owe it to your body to have sex, you owe it to your psyche to have sex and you almost certainly owe it to your relationship.

In a long-term relationship, wanting sex is a 'mind thing' as much as a physical imperative. The next time you sense a resistance to the idea of sex, remember the

*Here's an idea for you...*

**If you're feeling down, try having sex. Sex releases hormones that have an anti-depressant effect so it could prove a real comfort to you when you're blue. It's an especially powerful way to express painful emotions, and couples sometimes find that it helps them recover from traumatic experiences such as bereavement.**

words of Tom Hopkins, best-selling author of *How to Master the Art of Selling*, 'Winners almost always do what they think is the most productive thing possible at every given moment: losers never do.' Sometimes, he says, the most productive use of your time is to watch the sunset or talk to your spouse. Usually, I say, the most productive use of your time is having sex. Done well – with passion and enthusiasm – half an hour of sex is worth hours of doing just about anything else – it's the ultimate multitasking activity. It's not just good for your relationship; it's great for you too. When you're swithering about whether or not to go for it, reread this chapter and remember all that sex can do for you. Then ask, 'Am I winner or a loser?'

**Your mission**
To overcome a 'take it or leave it' attitude to sex.

**Your task**
Read the following every day for the next week and thereafter once a week.

**SEX DEFUSES STRESS**

'Progressive relaxation' is a relaxation technique that involves tensing and then relaxing muscles in a controlled manner throughout the body. After a while, it sends you to sleep. Orgasmic sex works in much the same way. (No sarky comments, please.) It also involves tensing and relaxing your muscles, but far more intensely. The result is that people with fulfilling sex lives are generally far less stressed, less anxious, less hostile and, bizarrely, far more likely to take responsibility for their own lives (one of the prime signs of a successful person, apparently).

**Read IDEA 44, *It's not all in your mind*, if you're bemused by where your libido's gone.**

*Try another idea...*

## SEX BOOSTS SELF-ESTEEM

Good sex makes us feel better about ourselves because it can be such an intimate experience. You're letting your soul out for a little play in front of another person, and it's a huge ego kick if they like what they see. It gives our personality a sense of completeness that we rarely experience unless we're particularly evolved human beings. Of course, if you don't receive wholehearted acceptance, the opposite happens and you feel rubbish. This is why you shouldn't have sex with people who don't seem to like you letting your soul out to play or, even worse, are so self-absorbed they don't seem to notice that's what you're doing. But, hey, that's a whole different book.

*'Sex is not the answer. Sex is the question. "Yes" is the answer.'*
ANONYMOUS

*Defining idea...*

## SEX IS THERAPEUTIC

The Chinese believe that you can treat everything from a cold to eczema with sex. One thing for sure, it's good for your heart both metaphorically and literally. One study looked at the sex lives of women who had been admitted to hospital following a heart attack. Of these, 65% reported that they experienced no sexual feelings or were unhappy with their sex lives in some way. When researchers asked women who were hospitalised for other, non heart-related conditions, only 24% reported having non-existent or poor quality sex lives.

## SEX IS CREATIVE

In an ideal world we'd all be scribbling away in diaries or expressing our emotions through dance and no doubt we'd be a happier, less repressed society for it. But who would feed the cat?

Seriously though, most of us don't make time to express our emotions or even to recognise them as they flit across our consciousness. During sex is a perfect time to get back in touch with the 'inner you'. As you touch each other, imagine you're expressing how you feel right at that moment. How are you feeling? Angry, sad, happy, secure, frustrated? Communicate this to your lover through your touch, words and actions. For some, this will appear scarier than the thought of dressing up in a nappy and parading down the High Street, and you're the ones who really need to experiment with sex as a creative act.

## SEX HELPS YOU LIVE LONGER

It's true. Studies have shown that those with a healthy sex life are more resistant to disease and the ill effects of stress. An orgasm boosts the body's white cell count (the cells that fight infection) by up to 20%. But note that we're talking about a happy sex life here. Miserable, joyless sex probably doesn't confer benefits, although no one has done the studies. We don't know why good sex works, but it's probably partly to do with the beneficial effects of having someone stroke you lovingly. Your immune system improves when you're caressed, stroked and hugged.

**Q** **Are you saying we should grit our teeth, think of the advantages and have sex when we don't feel like it?**

*How was it for you?*

**A** *Exactly. 'Feeling' like sex is a fragile flower that rarely blooms. Forget feeling like it, just do it. There are all sorts of complex psychological reasons why we go off having sex with our long-term partners. Allow this to happen and inertia will set in. This idea is aimed at reversing that mindset, which is why you have to read about the benefits of sex repeatedly. It's a brainwashing thing.*

**Q** **My partner and I are perfectly happy with doing it once a month or so. Are we damaging our health?**

**A** *If you and your partner are both totally happy with little or no sex, fine. But if there's any sort of discrepancy (and I guess you wouldn't be reading this if you were both happy), then work a bit harder at getting yourself in the mood more often. Think more about sex, do more to pleasure yourself, make your daily life as sensual as possible. If the problem is that your partner doesn't deliver what you need to enjoy sex, then you have to talk to them, but above all remember that sex is one of those things where 'use it or lose it' applies in spades.*

# Getting jiggy with your G-spot

**Think of the G-spot like Cliff Richard's sex appeal. It might not do much for you, but that doesn't mean it doesn't exist.**

It's generally accepted that it was Freud and the 50s who did for the G-spot.

Stimulation of this internal hot spot, situated just inside the vagina, can result in the so-called vaginal orgasm. But when Freud branded clitoral orgasms 'immature' and vaginal orgasms as superior he guaranteed that come the sexual revolution a whole swathe of stubborn women, relieved that they could come at all, weren't going to waste a precious moment fixating on an elusive vaginal orgasm and dissing their lovely clitoral ones because some dead bloke thought they weren't good enough.

The clitoral orgasm got to be the popular girl at the party while the vaginal orgasm languished in a corner. Even the sexologists gave up on her. Here's one example: 'It is clear that women only have one kind of climax – even though different climaxes brought about in different ways can feel different. And...this climax is brought about by one thing only – the arousal of the clitoris.'

Here's an idea for you... **If you want to be able to ignore the sensation of needing to pee while searching for your G-spot, empty your bladder beforehand and anything that comes out will be ejaculate.**

So, even if you were one of the 30% of women who claimed to come through penetration, the general opinion was that you were either misguided or showing off. Then came the 90s and it became fashionable to 'give bi a try' and a whole generation of young women went home from their girlfriends to teach their boyfriends what they'd learned. However, a lot of older, more sexually experienced women – through trial and error with their long-term male lovers – discovered that the G-spot was alive and kicking, but weren't making a fuss about it.

OK, sociology lesson over, but it's fascinating to think there are fashions in orgasm just like everything else. Anyway, here's what we think now. Most (if not all) women have a G-spot. Some people experience terrific sexual excitement from having their G-spot stimulated. Some feel a warm oozy feeling like listening to King's College carols at Christmas – and just about as sexually exciting. Some find G-spot stimulation intensely irritating. Some feel nothing much at all. And some feel an overwhelming need to pee that, depending on their sexual make-up, feels either unbearably uncomfortable or unbearably exciting. The only way you're going to find out if your G-spot is worth bothering with is to give it a go.

There's good and bad news for blokes who are reading this and getting excited at the thought of a female orgasm initiated by penetrative sex. The good news? This really is a case of size doesn't matter – the G-spot is situated within the first three inches of the vagina. The bad news? Humping away is going to miss the spot entirely. Your missus won't come from deep, hard thrusting in the time-honoured tradition of porn movies. It requires shallow penetration, skill and a bit of a concentration to hit the G-spot with your penis, much less bring her off in this way.

**For more ways to make the G-spot happy turn to IDEA 36, *The joy of shopping,* and IDEA 37, *Play away.***

*Try another idea...*

## WOMEN...

Squat and have a feel. The G-spot is situated on the front of the vaginal wall about a third to half way towards the cervix, a few inches inside. It feels slightly rough and is about a couple of centimetres across. Struggling? Feel for something that's more of a ridge than round. Pressing on the G-spot will feel spongy because what you're feeling through the skin of the vagina wall is the insulation that surrounds the urethra, which carries urine from your bladder to the outside world. The insulating sheath includes multiple glands that swell during sexual excitement and when stimulated in the right way will spurt out a clear fluid that emerges through the urethra just like pee. This is totally different in composition from pee and is, in fact, the so-called female ejaculate.

Many people don't like the idea of women ejaculating. And many of these people are women. But sisters relax. Embrace your bodily fluids. Even if you don't want to go the whole way, playing around with our G-spot is a pleasurable thing for most. Many people can get a big hit from just fiddling around down there. Many aren't men.

*'Sex pleasure in the woman is a kind of magic spell; it demands complete abandon; if words or movements oppose the magic of caresses the spell is broken.'*
MASTERTON and COLDWELL, *How to Drive Your Man Wild in Bed*

*Defining idea...*

## MEN...

Men who want to float their partner's love boat with some G-spot action might find using a finger rather than their penis is a lot less tiring. Have your partner sit or lie facing you, insert your index finger and press firmly repeatedly. You may have to go quite fast, but if she likes this get her to demonstrate first or you could do her damage. Also, try hooking your finger slightly as if beckoning and press repeatedly on the G-spot.

If you get bored and decide to employ your love wand in your quest, remember that shallow penetration is the only kind that works and imagine you're aiming for the navel. Rear entry positions are best; the 'spoon', where you both lie on your sides with him behind her, is easiest on both of you. Nothing happening? Try a vibrator that's specifically designed to hit the G-spot. Women may feel the need to pee during these manoeuvres, as stimulating the G-spot means you're pressing on the urethra. But stick with it, as it means you're getting close.

Is it worth it? Nearly all women enjoy having attention paid to the anterior wall of the vagina because of the huge number of nerve endings there. Becoming aware of how they react to different kinds of stimulation – manual, penile and plastic – can only improve your sexual repertoire of sensations. Just don't get hung up on it. Women don't need another body part to get neurotic about.

**Q    We stuck at it for ten minutes. Nothing much happened though I quite enjoyed it. Was that long enough?**

*How was it for you?*

*A    Plenty long enough for the first attempt. Try again when you're having a particularly long and animalistic session and you're very steamed up. The more excited you are the better. Performance pressure won't help, so buy a vibrator and experiment on your own.*

**Q    We couldn't find it. What are we doing wrong?**

*A    When you're searching for the G-spot together, plenty of foreplay is crucial. It swells when its owner is sexually excited and you can't find it otherwise. So, when she's well on the way to coming, apply firm, steady pressure to the G-spot. There's actually another hot spot just above the G-spot between it and the cervix. Try experimenting with the anterior wall of the vagina in general. You might be surprised at what you discover.*

# 11

# Paying for it

**Slut sex can be a turn-on for both of you.**

Both sexes can get a huge kick out of
acting out prostitution fantasies. This
explores our attitudes to power and control
(often erotically charged) and both sexes are able
to relish the freedom of imagining that they're
having no-holds-barred, no-strings-attached sex.

The 'client' gets the thrill of the clean transaction, of the freedom of asking for what he wants, of control, of being in charge. The 'whore' gets the visible proof that he values what she does in bed. (For the sake of clarity, I'm coming over all traditional and assuming 'he' is the client and 'she' the whore but, of course, this fantasy begs for role reversal. The powerful female client and the stud-for-hire can be just as much of a turn-on.)

This is one that definitely works better if you've both had a couple of drinks beforehand because alcohol removes the self-consciousness from role-playing, and for this idea to really work you both need to stay in character throughout.

Here's an idea for you... **There's an easy way to add a heightened sense of reality to the fantasy of paid-for sex: she keeps the money.**

## ACTING OUT

### 1 The Classic

Arrange to meet on a certain street corner at a certain time. Make sure there's not the slightest chance of it being mistaken for a red-light area or you might get more reality than you bargained for. She should dress as overtly sexily as she feels comfortable with in public; simply slipping off her knickers beforehand will give that added frisson. At the appointed hour, he pulls up in his car and asks whether she is available. She replies, 'For what?' Then he tells her in explicit detail. She comes back with the cost. Haggling or 'negotiating a price' can be a turn-on, and she shouldn't get in the car until the deal is done. You can now either drive back home and pretend it's her place or, if you're daring, use the car (somewhere private, of course, or again this game could get a bit too real).

### 2 The Pick-up

She's sitting at a hotel bar, looking sexy but demure. It helps if she adopts a slightly different look from usual – more make-up, hair slightly different, heels higher – a look that makes her feel unlike herself. She should make sure her underwear is brand new – nothing he's ever seen before. She should order a different drink from usual and adopt a different name and personality – the easier the new persona comes to her the more convincing this will be. The same applies to him: he should invent a new persona, too, and 'work it up'.

He approaches her and, although there may be some preliminary 'soft soap', eventually a conversation not unlike the one above has to take place. Maintain eye contact. It's sexier. When you're done head home (or better still, take a room). Don't talk overly much.

## 3 The Hotel Room

Book a hotel room and pay for it in advance.

She arrives first and changes – a wig if she can bear it, lingerie he's never seen before, heels, different perfume, negligée if she's uncomfortable strutting around near naked. Make the mood seductive with music and candles. She should psyche herself up – she's a high-class call girl and her job is to make him feel good. High-class call girls are paid a lot because they're brilliant actresses – so she should put her heart into it.

At last, he knocks on the door and she lets him in. Introduce yourselves by different names. Open a bottle of champagne. He can be nervous – that's still in chracter. But she must be confident and tease, flirt or be sexually voracious. She should read her client and take her clues from him (he, of course, has to act out his other side – the side that frequents prostitutes). She must make it clear she's here for one reason only – to give him the best sexual experience he's ever had. What would it take? What does he like? She should name her price and make it high. She's the ultimate indulgence. She's *expensive*. When the price has been agreed and she has the cash, lead him to the bed and get down to business. She should remember that this is her job and she's very, very good at it. If she can slip a few tricks in that he definitely won't be expecting, all the better. Maintain roles until the door closes behind him.

**Combine this with what you read in IDEA 15, *Something for the weekend*. Going away can be the perfect scenario for putting this idea into action.**

Try another idea...

*'You always pay for sex, but not always in cash.'*
ANONYMOUS

Defining idea...

How was it for you?

**Q  I think the paid-for-sex fantasy is distasteful. Am I being unduly prudish?**

A  *Women who charge for sex exert a powerful fascination for many people – but maybe not for you. However, I know from interviewing men talking about their sexual fantasies that the idea of being with a prostitute makes completely faithful men wonder, 'What if?' And women – even the most feminist – get an illicit thrill at the thought of breaking one of our society's strongest taboos and making themselves completely sexually available. Since in our culture women decide whom they'll sleep with and when, there's something powerfully erotic in subverting that societal law by pretending she has no choice but to offer herself as a sexual plaything to anyone who can afford her. The pretended helplessness is a huge turn-on for many women whether you approve or not. Turn the page if there's an issue in your past that makes thinking about prostitution unpleasant or even painful, and I'm sorry it's offended you. But if not, dip a toe in. What offends us, pushes our boundaries, and that is powerfully erotic.*

**Q  We enjoyed the sex, but the lead up was a bit awkward. Any ideas?**

A  *Try again. Introduce some new elements to the initial pick-up or try reversing roles. Promise to do all you can to support each other in the make-believe. No giggling or sniggering. Also, next time promise each other you'll each do one thing that the other one isn't expecting during the encounter. After all, you're supposed to be strangers and you'd surprise each other in real life. If none of these suggestions work, then maybe this just isn't your scenario. Move on.*

# 12

# The love's there, but the lust's gone AWOL

**Hey sexual pioneer! Yes, we're talking to you.**

If you're a baby boomer in a sexual relationship that's lasted more than nine years, then you're breaking new sexual ground. The human race doesn't have much practice of doing what you're doing. We simply don't know how to do long-term relationships.

As Dr Alan Altman writes in *Making Love the Way We Used To, Or Better,* 'Many people are disappointed when they can't re-create those early thrilling feelings. [But] We don't really have many examples of how to keep a 25 plus year marriage alive sexually. At the turn of a century a 47-year-old male was considered old.'

Are we programmed to get bored with a long-term partner? There's a persuasive argument that we are. Psychologists believe that one reason we go off sex with long-term lovers is the powerful anti-incest taboos that are part of nearly every culture. Basically, in a 'functional' family, brothers and sisters who are brought up

Here's an idea for you...

**A long-term sexual relationship will go in cycles – sometimes strong, sometimes fading. Sexual desire is something you can rekindle, but make sure your partner is singing from the same hymn sheet. When the first flush of lust passes, it won't come back without will and compassion from each of you for the other.**

together don't fancy each other despite incredible proximity. However, brothers and sisters who are brought up apart often do. It may be that if we live too long with someone of the opposite sex, we stop reacting to their sexual charisma. This is why we must never get too cosy with each other or allow our boundaries to become too melded.

We long for the thrills of the beginning of the relationship. We yearn for the time when our partners were mad for us. Sometimes we want it so much that we move onto another relationship to get the kicks. So there's the bad news. Your challenge is to decide what to do about it. Interview the sexual pioneers – women and men who have successfully lived with each other for many years – and they talk touchingly about the power that sexuality shared with one partner over many years can hold. One woman interviewed by writer Brigid McConville in her book *The Secret Life* says, 'We have been together for so long, when I look at him not just as my ageing bloke but as the man who made love to me on the beach in Greece, on the train across Europe, and tied to the bedposts in a hotel in Spain. No one else has those intimate memories, just us. No one else knows what he is capable of. It's a bond so strong it's a bit like having children together: nothing can change the history of our intimacy and what we have made and shared and I can conjure up images of us making love together any time I like.'

How do you get to the place where a lifetime's worth of loving experience informs your view of your lover? In a nutshell: don't get boring and don't get bored. Ask yourself some hard questions. If you love your partner but are no longer excited by them, reverse it. How exciting are you? How passionate are you? Would you fancy yourself? Do you feel alive?

**For more on remaining your own person and keeping a spark between you turn to IDEA 39,** *Let a woman be a woman and a man be a man*, **and IDEA 47,** *Developing sexual mystique.*

*Try another idea...*

Are you passionate about work or your interests? Do you have any interests? Are you enthusiastic about your children, your friends and the things you talk about with them?

What projects do you have on the backburner for the future that excite you?

If you're drawing a blank here, it's time to get back your passion for life. There's absolutely no way you'll get it back for your partner without it. And be warned, moving onto another partner in the hope of regaining your passion for life will work in the short term, but never in the long term. This isn't always the complete answer to the 'love but no lust' dilemma, but it's the first crucial step.

*'Anyone who knows Dan Quayle knows that he would rather play golf than have sex any day.'*
MARILYN QUAYLE, responding to charges that her husband had an affair while on a golf holiday

*Defining idea...*

53

*How was it for you?*

**Q   How do you rekindle your passion for life when you have no time?**

A   *If you don't make time for this it means it's not your priority, which is a bit sad. One simple way that was taught to me by a very wise woman with five kids and a work schedule to make you cry, is to down all tools – whether computer, iron or dishwasher – at 8.30 p.m. each night. That means the house is often a mess and I sometimes have to rise early, sit in the car to get away from the children and finish work I should have done the night before. But, and it's a big but, I get time nearly every night to chill out on my own (usually), with my bloke (often) or with friends (occasionally). Yes, even on a week night. Just find an hour a day at first to get back your juice and take it from there. At first, you'll be twiddling your thumbs and thinking, 'I really should clean the bathroom.' However, soon you'll be yearning for your 'hour' like water in the desert.*

**Q   Our sex is fine, but it's just not earth shattering. Why not?**

A   *It won't always be, but you can feel as sexually alive as you did at the beginning of the relationship, even more so. The secret is not to rely on spontaneous desire. If you want exciting sex, you have to become an expert at making it happen. The reasons we go off sex when it's proscribed by society and not 'forbidden', i.e. when we're 'settled down', are huge and complex – we've just touched on them here. Fight your conditioning. There are plenty of ways to combat sexual inertia, but the best bit of advice is to stop waiting for fireworks to just happen. Think about sex, reach for sex, want sex, relish sex. Use it to give life texture and make it fun.*

# 13

# Coming over all touchy-feely

**Learn to express sensuality with your whole body.**

Think of ways you can actively be more aware of your bodies and new sensations together. Here are some ideas to keep you both sensually orientated throughout the next week.

**STEP 1**

Showering together is one of those things you do at the beginning of a relationship that tails off as the mortgage gets bigger and your hair gets greyer. Give your lover a surprise this week. Wait until it's good and steamy in there. Strip off, step in and start soaping them down.

I recommend showers rather than baths as although I'm seriously addicted to candlelit baths, when you're getting wet together I think there's something more intimate about showering than bathing. Probably because the sound of the shower cuts you off from the outside world, makes talk less likely and forces you to get physical together. But only, of course, if your shower is a powerful one. A pathetic dribble where you are both edging the other one out to get a share of the water is a

Here's an idea for you... **Men: instead of using your hands to massage her body, use the sensitive inside of your forearms – it will feel new for both of you.**

dead loss. If you're looking for a good reason to install a decent shower – make it your love life.

Note for women: put on some gorgeous wispy underwear and step into the shower with him when he's not expecting it. Naked's good. Naked's great. But the feel (and the look!) of the wet fabric plastered against your slick body and the rush he'll get from pushing it aside to get at you should make for a different kind of experience.

## STEP 2

Look for different ways to surprise each other with unexpected sensations:

- Wear something different from the norm. If you sleep naked, try silk pyjama bottoms. If you always wear a nightdress, change to a simple white cotton brief and vest set.

- Introduce a feather into lovemaking. Ask your lover to close their eyes and trail it over their bare skin. Some people hate it, some love it, but it sensitises bare skin and makes it more reactive to other stimulation.

- Heat up a towel with a hairdryer while your lover's bathing and offer it to them as they come out. A toasty hot towel is delicious, unexpected and will get you brownie points for thoughtfulness. Make sure they do the same for you.

- Take an ice cube and rub it over your lover's bare back or nipples while you're making love until it melts. Take in the sensations, from shock through enjoyment. Couple with some gentle slaps if you want to get kinky. Heat then cold is very sensitising.

## STEP 3

Marilyn Monroe's sexual signature note had nothing to do with her looks (her partner couldn't see her) or his degree of sexual satisfaction (he didn't even come) and everything to do with the electrifying power that touch can have on your average adult male, deprived as he is of all-over, deeply sensual, touch.

Turn to IDEA 34, *The love bath*, for some more things to do in the shower. IDEA 45, *Pressure – it's not a dirty word*, gives details of massage techniques.

*Try another idea...*

Marilyn, so the story goes, would ask her lover to lie on his front and remain very, very still. Once he was in position she'd straddle him from behind and whisper in his ear that he was going to help her to come. Then she'd liberally apply oil on his back and her body and start slithering up and down on him, rubbing her vulva and clitoris against his back and buttocks, over and over again, finding just the right spot to grind her hips to give her the right pressure, whispering all the time about how turned on she was, how hot she was, how close she was…until, finally, inevitably, she came. The bloke probably quite enjoyed it too.

Clever Marilyn – what's more likely to make your lover mad for you than letting them know they're driving you mad with lust, while ensuring they get to have a nice little lie down at the same time?

*'I'm suggesting we call sex something else, and it should include everything from kissing to sitting close together.'*
SHERE HITE, sex researcher

*Defining idea...*

57

Women: try your own version of the Marilyn manoeuvre.

Men: to reawaken your sense of touch (the point of this exercise), you could massage your lover while asking her to stay perfectly still. Once she's melting use your imagination, and her body, to find a way of bringing yourself to the point of orgasm without her having to lift a finger. Extra points if you manage to come, but if you don't, make sure she does.

How was it for you?

**Q**  **My partner finds this sort of stuff excruciating. He even finds taking a shower together a bit irritating rather than interesting. What can I do?**

*A*  *He's a man deeply in denial of something, although I've no idea what. Some of the scenarios in this book can make men feel very self-conscious and a bit foolish. It's a difficult one. What he has to understand is that it's not about him – it's about you. Is he prepared to give a little to make you happy? That should be reason enough for him to give it a go. Be patient and in the meantime treat yourself sensually every chance you get. Ask him to share in that with you. Eventually you'll break him down.*

**Q**  **This is all very nice but does it really help improve our sex life?**

*A*  *You're right. Waving a feather over your skin isn't going to produce any thundering orgasms. But becoming more aware of the power of touch will make you more sensitive during lovemaking and more likely to experiment. Following these ideas or similar ones will open up communication between you. You'll be a better lover. And that's guaranteed to improve your sex life.*

# 14

# Surprise!

**Isn't it time you got in touch with your creative side?**

Laura Corn, author of '101 Nights of Grrreat Sex', has based her considerable best-selling success on one simple concept: the importance of the surprise factor. Each of her 101 suggestions depends on the fact that your partner doesn't have a clue what sexual delight you're planning.

It's a clever gimmick and it works. Surprise your lover sexually every week for a year and you can bet your bootee you won't be collecting any 'boring in bed' prizes. Encouraging the element of surprise in your sex life will keep you young and playful, keep you feeling cherished and appreciated and keep your lover crazy for you.

*Here's an idea for you...* **Do something slightly different *every* time you make love. Throw in an element of surprise. Mixing it up will become second nature after a few weeks and the payoff will make it worthwhile.**

A little bit of effort to surprise your lover with a new technique, seduction, outfit or behaviour reaps huge improvements. As long as it's something unexpected, the surprise can be whatever you like. It can be filthy, funny, sweet and romantic or it can be more embarrassing than karaoke night down your local.

## WHY SURPRISE WORKS

Some of your surprises will be easy to organise. Some will take more planning. You might spend an hour (or more) setting up a gorgeous seduction for your mate, which is a lot I grant you, but the end result (and this is no exaggeration) will be burned into the hard drive of their memory for the rest of their life. Great sex has that sort of effect on us.

But even more unforgettable for your mate than the great sex you'll enjoy is how loved they'll feel. Men, just as much as women (in fact, if the psychologists are to be believed, even *more* than women), are delighted by the proof that someone wants them so much that they'll put thought and effort into their seduction. All of us love to feel special.

## WHAT DOES IT TAKE FOR IT TO WORK?

It takes both of you to commit to the idea. You will only want to put effort into thrilling your partner if you feel they're going to make the same effort for you.

It will be especially hard to have a boring sex life if you combine this idea with IDEA 17, *Learn the art of kaizen.*

*Try another idea...*

I recommend Laura Corn's book (mentioned above) because she gives you lots of ideas and she gives you structure. The surprise element can't be spontaneous, at least not at first. If we don't plan, we just get lazy and don't bother. You're aiming to give your lover a 'guaranteed surprise', if you see what I mean. In other words, although they'll be able to look forward to being surprised, they won't know what they're looking forward to.

If you don't want to spring for Corn's book, then in the immortal words of Fleetwood Mac, 'Go your own way.' Or simply customise some of the following suggestions to get the ball rolling:

*'We want to know how to turn our mates on. We want them to know what turns us on. We'd like more variety...more foreplay...more surprises...more interest...new tricks...and, once in a while, somebody else should do all the work!'*
LAURA CORN

*Defining idea...*

**For her**

- He's in the shower. Wait until it's good and steamy in there and then slip in beside him wearing your flimsiest, sheerest underwear. If there's one thing more likely to turn him on than you naked, it's wet, clinging wisps of material. (Blokes could try this, too, but it has to be silk boxers – soggy, cotton Y-fronts just don't cut it.)

- On your next date, you can keep your coat on. Well, you don't want the whole restaurant to know you're naked underneath. Just him.

**For him**

- Buy her half a case of her favourite wine (a dozen bottles is classier, but might be too much of a demand on your imagination). Around the neck of each, place a sealed envelope containing details of where and when you're going to drink it together. These are IOUs of pleasure. Let your imagination run riot.

- One night when you're getting amorous in a lovey-dovey sort of way, suddenly flip personality – change the whole atmosphere. From Dr Jekyll to Mr Hyde. Stop smiling. Get mean. Overcome her. Tie her wrists to the headboard and blindfold her. Now you can do whatever you like, but if you want to give her a night to remember (and especially if she's still really pissed off with you), go down on her until she stops cursing and starts begging.

- Spend an hour or so pleasuring her sensually, such as oral sex, washing her hair, painting her toenails, applying body lotion to every inch of her skin or holding her and stroking her hair until she falls asleep. Don't allow her to do a thing for you in return.

**Q** **I tried getting a bit rough, but my wife hated it. How should I approach this now?**

*A* *The all-important point of this whole surprise thing is that it shouldn't come as a surprise to your mate. You need to talk beforehand and agree on the general concept of bringing the element of surprise into your lovemaking. If it came out of the blue, being tied up could easily be too much. Surprise her with a few less extreme ideas, then talk to her about her feelings on bondage to establish whether the bondage per se was the problem or whether it was your personality change that shocked her.*

**Q** **I bought my wife some expensive lingerie and laid it out on the bed. She laughed and said she'd save it for 'a big occasion'. What did I do wrong?**

*A* *She probably felt pressurised. Be careful not to make the surprise simply about the lingerie. Make it about* her *in the lingerie. In fact, forget about the lingerie for a while and concentrate on giving her a massage next time she's tired. Surprise her with romance and thoughtfulness for a few weeks, then explain how you're trying to improve your relationship. If she seems chuffed, suggest that maybe she could surprise you with the lingerie sometime, if she feels like it. Remember: no pressure. Throw it over to her then continue with the romance, the thoughtfulness and the occasional move in bed that she's not expecting. Soon she'll be joining in.*

How was it for you?

# 15

# Something for the weekend

**Time spent away together intensifies your experiences. Making sex the focus of your break will revitalise your love life.**

Bridget Jones turned the romantic 'mini-break' into a joke, but if your relationship has been in a bit of a slump, a few days away from it all really is a perfect chance to recharge your sexual batteries.

Prioritising sex rather than, say, sightseeing or gastro-pubbing, will fire up your love life for possibly months afterwards. The reason is that a new place lets you reinvent yourselves. You'll be more daring and more focussed on each other. And if you have any problem areas, you can plan to sort them out them over the weekend.

Here are some ideas for solving two common relationship problems during a typical two-day break. Use them as a model to write out your own 'prescription for love'. (Sorry, couldn't help myself.)

Here's an idea for you... **Get a room and experiment with those 'pay-for-sex' fantasies that you've always meant to try together.**

**Predicament:** You're turning into 'just good friends'.
**Goal:** Re-establish yourselves as lovers.

It's oh-so-very easy to get into the rut of being good companions rather than red-hot lovers. Everything about your break should be geared to remind you of the sensual things in life. Don't make it about catching up on culture, unless you happen to get fantastically turned on by modern art. Think long, boozy lunches in shady cafes and then back to the hotel bed for a siesta because it's too damn hot to do much else. Think Spain or Italy.

The sexual focus of the weekend should be on rediscovering your excitement in each other and forging the bond between you as lovers. You could:

**Day 1.** Build excitement. Kiss, touch each other up, grope, spend hours on foreplay but break out of your rut by not having sex. Pretend that you are new lovers who aren't ready to move on to the sexual stage of a relationship. Be a little shy – shut the bathroom door. Take time with your appearance. See each other as you did in your first days together. Work on feelings of compassion and affection for your lover – see them through the same rose-coloured specs that you did in the beginning. Be determined to find them deeply endearing, no matter how much they were irritating you yesterday. Allow yourself to be charmed.

**Day 2.** Resolve to do something you'll never forget. You can probably remember vivid details of your lovemaking during the first six months of your relationship. It's the last six years that are tricky. After the build-up of yesterday, create new shared memories of sex that will stay with both of you when you get home and fuel desire when the rut beckons again. Use the new location to the max. Move mirrors in your hotel room so that you can see yourselves while you have sex. Throw your lover against a wall in a tiny cobbled street. Slip away from the lights and have it off on the beach.

**Predicament:** Your love life is predictable.
**Goal:** To regain the sparkle.

**If getting away is a problem, try IDEA 51, *Fantasy destinations*.**

Try another idea...

Usually when sex is predictable, you have temporarily lost that special feeling of closeness that gives you the confidence to initiate new things and explore your sexuality. Choose a location where it will be easy to relax and spend time talking with each other. Avoid anything that involves a lot of hassle or even excitement, so forget backpacking through Eastern Europe. Think quiet auberge in the South of France or luxurious English country house.

**Day 1.** Create intimacy. Turn your hotel bedroom into a sensual sanctuary. Take oils and candles from home. Spend a couple of hours bathing, showering and massaging each other before dinner. Don't rush into sex (or if you do, maintain the sensual touching afterwards). Live in the moment. Rediscover each other. Hold hands. Maintain eye contact as much as possible. Spend an hour talking about your feelings about work, family, friends and your relationship. Your aim is to make your lover feel cherished and 'listened to'.

**Day 2.** Break the patterns. Each write three things you'd like to try on a piece of paper. Think about this in advance so you've any props to hand. Take turns to fulfil each other's wishes. If you find this giving too hard, make it a game – be each other's sex slave.

'*When you do something kinky, it's like, yes, the mango sex. We'll always remember the mango sex...It wasn't even that good, but we remember it. And that's the key – the remembering.*'
BETH LAPIDES, American comedian

Defining idea...

67

*How was it for you?*

**Q It's fine when we're away and for about a week afterwards. Then the lovey-dovey feelings go and it's back to business as usual. How can we keep that lovin' feeling?**

A *Make 'change for change's sake' your mantra in every aspect of your life together. It serves to make you more spontaneous with each other. For instance, moving the position of your bed can subconsciously remind you to keep things fresh in the bedroom. As can something as simple as swapping sides of the bed. Who made the rule that he always sleeps on the left? Do you always eat dinner at the table? Then have a picnic in front of the TV. Does one of you take responsibility for cleaning the car? Then the other one should do it for a month. If you're constantly making small subtle changes in your everyday life, you'll automatically bring this into the bedroom – or on the kitchen table if you're really entering into the spirit of things. When change is an everyday part of your life, it's easier to suggest something new sexually to your partner.*

**Q It's difficult for us to get time away. Are there any alternatives?**

A *Fine, just set aside two days together at home, and work out your timetable of love. And if you really can't find the time to be at home together, you've got a big problem. Very few people have reasons so genuine that they can't find a way past them if they're motivated enough. If you're not motivated enough, that's your problem. Talk about it first.*

# 16

# Think kink

**Remember: we don't always get what we want.
But we can ask.**

Your mission, should you choose to accept
it, is to ask your partner to try
something you're convinced has never occurred
to them. This idea is a generic 'how to' on
asking for this something, be it group sex,
dogging, fisting, voting nationalist or whatever.

## STATING THE OBVIOUS

If you want to try something out of the norm, then you'll have to communicate it
to your lover either verbally or physically.

1. Butter them up first by faking a midlife crisis. Tell them you're worried that
   they'll leave you – couples are splitting up everywhere (give examples). Do this
   in a light-hearted way over a bottle of wine or in a worried way after faking
   moodiness that has them wondering what's wrong. I recommend the former,

but hey, it's your relationship. Tell them that although your love life is fine, you feel you've been complacent and you don't want them to get bored. Modify this basic script depending on your lover's gullibility levels but you get the basic idea – you make it your problem, not theirs. And then you make some changes to your love life.

2.  Once you've mixed it up a little and you're regularly trying new things, suggest a modest first step on the way to what you want. If you want them to whip you with a cat of nine tails, then suggesting you experiment with a little mild pain via dripping candle wax is a good start.

3.  Work up to the real deal. Be patient. Six months' patient if necessary.

*Here's an idea for you...*

If you're still shy of asking for what you really want, remember that the taboo of today is the norm of tomorrow. Rejoice in the thought of being a sexual pioneer, and pity all those blokes who went through the fifties longing for a blowjob but who were too afraid to ask in case they were thought to be perverts.

**NEVER FORGET**

The secret in persuading your lover to do something kinky that you want and they aren't particularly interested in is to make it clear that it's *them* doing the kinky thing that you're interested in, not the kinky thing itself. Use imagination, tact and flattery to find a way to make this obvious.

Right: 'Your bum looks amazing in rubber.'
Wrong: 'All I can think of is Michelle Pfeiffer in that Cat Woman outfit.'

Remember that the secret is *always* to make your lover feel special and to convince them how special they are to you. You'd be quite amazed at the things that some people can persuade others to do with this terribly simple strategy. But I've seen the police reports.

## HOW NOT TO DO IT

I received a letter once from a man who couldn't understand why his new girlfriend wouldn't join him and his five best friends naked in a sauna for a beer. It turned him on so much and his ex-wife hadn't had a problem with it. Letting his mates leer at her and compare her with his previous bird must have been an alluring prospect for the new girlfriend! He was clearly not as interested in women *per se* as in their willingness to get naked in front of his mates. Something told me that here was a man with a lot of disappointment ahead of him.

**The last word:** Most sex lives benefit from including a few of the minor elements from some of the major fetishes. So, give it a go and if it's not you, don't try it again.

Try another idea...

Stuck for a kink to practice with? For inspiration turn to IDEA 21, *Bringing up the rear*, and IDEA 31, *Bunty and Daisy rather than Sadie and Maisie.*

Defining idea...

'[Kinky sex] is not about giving up "normal" sex, adopting a new "lifestyle", joining a "community" or becoming a "freak". It's about making sex hotter. It's about giving voice to your darker, maybe even slightly disturbing desires by exploring new sensations, playing make-believe and other mind games. It's about making kink a part of your everyday sex life...OK maybe just your weekend and holiday sex life.'
EM and LO, Sex gurus on nerve.com and authors of *The Big Bang*

How was
it for
you?

**Q    I want to get involved in dogging. Just watching other couples. I've mentioned it to my wife a few times, but she's not keen. What's my next move?**

A    *I have little sympathy with the bullying lover – and I fear you're one. Sexual bullies always play variations of this one theme: 'I love my partner. I really do. It's just always been my dearest sexual fantasy to watch group sex in a car park and damn it, she just isn't interested.' Sexual bullies always start with 'I love you' and end with 'If you don't do it, I'll find someone else who will.' So, if you're heading in that direction, think carefully about what that says about you.*

**Q    When does kinky become a problem?**

A    *If your lover starts expressing a wish for you to shave off your pubic hair, walk on their back in stilettoes and stick Smarties up their bum, then your job is to decide whether this a lover who wants you to add some spice to their sex life or whether the shaving, stilettoes and Smarties are an absolute prerequisite to having good sex with you (or anyone else). If it's the latter, you've got a fetishist on your hands and you have to decide whether you want that fetish to be a constant factor in your love life. If you can accept and incorporate your lover's kinks, they'll love you for it. I mean really love you for it. There are few things more devoted than the fetishist who is lucky enough to come across a lover who tolerates their obsession. But if it's something you want only occasionally, you have to be strong about your boundaries.*

# 17

# Learn the art of kaizen

**Kaizen is a Japanese concept that means, 'Small changes, big differences.' It can revolutionise your love life.**

Psychologists say that if you want to keep dementia at bay you need to keep your brain on its toes. Your brain operates on well-worn grooves and you should break them to improve your chances of staying mentally alert.

You probably always brush your teeth in the way you perfected in childhood, but if you surprise your brain by brushing your teeth with the other hand, you'll force it to work harder and stay fresher. Changing your routine just slightly – taking a new route to work, kissing friends when you meet rather than hugging them, eating your main meal at noon – will give you a different perspective, a new way of looking at things. Mixing it up will do the same for your sex life.

*Here's an idea for you...*

**Ban yourself from coming in your 'normal' way for a month. You'll have to work harder for results, but you'll be forced to be more inventive.**

Promise yourself that the next time you make love you will, as far as possible, work on the rule of difference. If you always start with kissing, try flipping your lover over and massaging their shoulders instead; if you prefer to be on top, then lie on your back; if you always come first, come second; if you almost always initiate sex, allow your lover to choose the time and place next time. You'll feel resistance, as your instincts will be to follow the same old pattern, but fight it. Let's cut to the chase: absolutely nothing – infidelity, children, the clap – is more ruinous to your love life than shagging more or less the same way more or less all the time. Both of you need to try to make sex different every time you do it. Obviously not completely different, but just a little bit different from the last time or, better still, the half a dozen times before that. There are hundreds of different ways to stimulate your partner with your mouth and hands – try them. Or groan 'no' if you always groan 'yes'. Or grab a soft scarf and run it between your partner's legs before rubbing them through the material. Anything at all to reassure your partner that you're not operating on automatic pilot.

*and another...*

**Look at every household object with renewed interest. Incorporate some of them into your lovemaking if possible – without frightening the horses.**

*Try another idea...*

**Turn to IDEA 30, *Assume the position*, for some ideas on jazzing up the 'old faithful' positions.**

As a rule of thumb:

1. Do something you haven't done in the last month or so every single time you make love.

2. Don't come in a certain position if you can remember exactly when you last came that way.

*'It's OK to laugh in the bedroom so long as you don't point.'*
WILL DURST, satirist

*Defining idea...*

**Q   The first and most important difference I'd like is for my wife to make the first move. If I wait for her to initiate sex, I'll wait forever. Why's that?**

*How was it for you?*

*A   Check your own responses first. Has your wife ever kissed you, approached you for a cuddle or held your hand when you just weren't in the mood? What did you do? Move away? Men often wish that their partner would initiate sex more, but what they really mean is initiate sex when they vaguely fancy it. Not, of course, when they're immersed in the cricket, which would be annoying. And annoyed is what your wife feels when you leap on her while she's sorting laundry. Men are generally terrific at bouncing back from rejection because most tend to get lots of practice in adolescence, and they're also willing to put up with their partner taking a moment to get on their sexual wavelength. Women – much more thin-skinned – take that original hesitation on your part as outright rejection and turn away. Perhaps for good. Be responsive when she's tactile, even if*

75

there's no chance of it progressing to sex. Her reaching for your hand while you're shopping could be the beginning of foreplay that isn't consummated until after dinner. If you do all of the above and respond to every twitch of her affectionate nature, then you'll have to explain to her that always taking the initiative is making you feel like you're harassing her. Ask her to surprise you just once in the upcoming month. Don't pressurise her and keep talking openly and gently.

**Q    Isn't this kaizen exhausting?**

A    If it's treated as a game, it's fun. More importantly, it will make you focus on your sexuality, and anytime you do that, your sex life will nearly always improve.

# 18

# Building bridges

**How can a woman come just like a man?**

*Women — if you could come as easily as your man, wouldn't you want to have sex more often? Men — if she came as easily as you did, wouldn't you be grateful?*

A ton of foreplay is, of course, vital. Oral sex is, of course, important. Candlelit dinners, lots of chat and making an effort for each other are critical for a long-standing, ever-loving relationship. But sometimes it's Monday night, you have an early start in the morning, you've had a long hard day and you just want for both of you to come with the minimum of effort.

As the Hite Report – the most exhaustive description of female sexuality available – tells us, the great majority of women need clitoral stimulation with either hand or vibrator if they're going to come during penetrative sex. Still the ideal persists that we should all be multiorgasmic by penile insertion. Frankly, it's rubbish. Thrusting the penis into the vagina is anatomically the same thing as pulling on a man's balls. You could make a man come eventually by this method – every tug would move the skin on the upper tip of the penis so eventually he might get enough stimulation – but boy, would it take a while. And for some men it would never work. The only hope for the vast majority of women is to get used to coming during penile penetration through clitoral stimulation.

Here's an idea for you... **Contract your vaginal muscles (PC muscles) as you approach orgasm. This will help bring on your orgasm and will also help you when you stop clitoral stimulation. Eventually, the contractions may be enough to power you into orgasm with no further clitoral stimulation. A few dirty words whispered in your ear won't hurt.**

According to the irresistibly direct D. Claire Hutchins in her almost as irresistibly titled *5 Minutes to Orgasm: Every Time You Make Love*, 'Millions of women enjoy orgasm during intercourse by using additional stimulation of the clitoris. The question should not be is this wrong? Can this be fixed? The question should be, why do we keep asking such a stupid question in the first place? Why resort to everything in the book, from scented candles and bubble baths, extensive analysis and sex therapy to make orgasm happen any other way. Ladies – let's move on. If the thought of touching yourself in front of your partner scares you, you'll have to get over it.'

Bravo D. Claire Hutchins. However, women and men do persist in feeling that they'd like to come from the same thrusting stimulation. And there is a way to do it: bridging. And what you're building is a 'bridge' between clitoral and penile stimulation. The bridge manoeuvre means simply using clitoral stimulation – which most women need to orgasm – to bring the woman to the very edge of coming, then desisting and the woman coming following a few thrusts more from the man. This is a three-step process that anyone can learn, although it takes practice. Personally speaking, if you get to step two and come that way, you'll still be in a good place.

### STEP 1: ADOPT THE POSITION

Find a position that allows maximum clitoral stimulation. It can be the missionary position or any other as long as your hand stimulates your clitoris. Best is the big mama of quick female orgasm: you straddle your partner, pull aside your labia and lean forward so that your clitoris rubs directly against his pelvic bone or sit upright so that you can masturbate your clitoris while on top of him.

**If you have trouble knowing what to fantasise about (it happens!), turn to IDEA 50, Dream time.**

*Try another idea...*

## STEP 2: BRING YOUR MIND INTO PLAY

You're on top (or underneath, or hanging off the ceiling pendant, whatever rocks your world), writhing about, touching yourself. Feel yourself getting closer to orgasm? No? OK, time to bring fantasy into the act. With fantasy, you stop worrying about your stomach wobbling, the kids' lost homework, whether he's getting bored or not or whether you are. With fantasy, you concentrate on sex. With fantasy, you're the star of the show, the focus of the action – and you're gorgeous. Or as American humorist Nora Ephron put it, 'In my fantasy, no one loves me for my mind.' Concentrate on achieving your orgasm.

Shut your eyes. Forget about your bloke if necessary. Don't stop until you come, if you want to bridge...

## STEP 3: BRIDGING

Take yourself to the very edge of orgasm and then stop the clitoral stimulation. Bring yourself off by grinding yourself against his body. This is partly a mental thing. When you believe you're going to come through penetration only, it's more likely that you will.

*'Women can't alter the physiology in order to conform to what is expected of us, so we adopt countless strategies to reconcile reality with expectations, including faking orgasm. But who loses? Women do, and so do men. Instead of faking it, let's just accept our bodies and move on. Let's adjust.'*
D. CLAIRE HUTCHINS, American writer

*Defining idea...*

79

How was it for you?

**Q  I tried this but it hasn't worked yet. Any ideas?**

A  *Masturbate more. Fine-tuning your sexual response by learning how to come as effectively as possible through masturbation is essential for most women wanting to come during penetration. If you do masturbate yourself to orgasm, then time yourself. How long from dead cold to orgasm? Between two to four minutes? Yup, that's normal. This is the average (just like men). If it's longer, keep practising until you're under the four minutes. Then use this three-minute-something orgasm and experiment with the bridging techniques. Sorry if it sounds clinical and not very romantic. It is a bit competitive, a bit pressurised and a bit performance orientated. A bit like what sex is like for a bloke, in fact. And that is the aim: to come efficiently and effectively every single time you have sex. Fabulous.*

**Q  Why is masturbation such a big deal? Can't my man stimulate me?**

A  *No, it's not about your man massaging you. Studies show that failure to orgasm is five times higher among women who never masturbate than among the rest of women; that out of approximately 10% of women who never orgasm, 95% have also never masturbated; that women who masturbate more come more often with their partners. I could go on...Just try it.*

# 19

# When your sex drives are out of sync

**Looking for a mate? Choose someone with roughly the same sex drive. Oh, sorry, you thought you had.**

Every relationship goes through periods when one person wants sex more than the other — you're exhausted but your partner has one thing pretty obviously on their mind or vice versa.

**ANY OF THE FOLLOWING FAMILIAR?**

**'I just don't want sex any more'**
This doesn't mean that you're always going to dread sex or that you won't regain your libido. There's nothing wrong with you either. What's far more likely is that your priorities have shifted and something else – job, kids, financial worries – is draining all your juice. Or it could be that for you sex is a demonstration of your closeness, but you feel distant from your partner: 'We're miles apart, but he/she still

Here's an idea for you... **The defining difference between couples having lots of sex and couples having virtually none is often a sense of playfulness. Play strip poker. Play Twister. Play doctors and nurses. Go to the cinema and have a snog. Do anything that means you have fun and you'll almost inevitably rekindle passion.**

wants sex.' If you're one of those people who when single always preferred having sex with someone you had a connection with, why would you change because you're in a long-term relationship? But as we all know in a long-term relationship, you're not always completely in tune mentally with your partner.

Whether you're stressed or feeling distant, the solution is the same. Get closer. Talk to your partner and explain how you're feeling. Spend time holding each other. Create spaces in your life to do this. Switch the TV off and cuddle up in front of the fire. Go to bed half an hour earlier for 'duvet time'. Spend time being physically and emotionally close and eventually you'll want sex more often. It might not be great at first, but eventually you should reach a place where your libidos are more closely in sync again.

**'My partner doesn't want me anymore'**
Are you sure that this isn't more that they don't want sex at the same time as you? It's truly astonishing to me the number of men who report being hurt and resentful following repeated rejection from a wife who falls asleep by nine-thirty most nights. Yet after a minute of careful questioning, it turns out they've never made the mental leap between her exhaustion and the fact that while he's lying in front of the telly, she's more often than not pottering around folding clothes, loading the

dishwasher or tidying up the day's debris. You have to be equally well rested for your libidos to get back in sync.

Don't hassle your partner for penetrative sex. Do hassle them for physical intimacy. You don't have the right to demand sex from your partner, but in a loving relationship, you are entitled to expect physical comfort and cherishing. And the latter makes the former a hell of a lot more likely. Increase physical intimacy, have just a little more sex and wait out your partner's lost libido. With patience and (loving) perseverance, you can help them find it again.

**Tiredness can be a passion killer, as can children. See IDEA 44, It's not all in your mind.**

*Try another idea...*

*'I am open to the guidance of synchronicity, and do not let expectations hinder my past.'*
DALAI LAMA

*Defining idea...*

How was
it for
you?

**Q    It feels wrong to have sex when I don't enjoy it. What should I do?**

*A    The most basic advice is to be sure to have an orgasm every time you make
love – I'm prepared to bet that at the moment you're not. Masturbate after
he comes (leave the bed if you're too shy, but think about why on earth
you should be), buy a vibrator or retrain your husband in a gentle way. Keep
having sex, but make sure there's always a payback for you. Sure, sex can
be great without an orgasm but it should happen on the minority not the
majority of occasions. Otherwise, of course, you'll be bored and you're
naturally going to resent him deep down somewhere.*

**Q    I've tried being patient. We're doing lots of cuddling and kissing.
We're also having a bit more sex, but although she seems to think
it's enough, I want it to be the way it used to be for us. How can I
recapture that?**

*A    Time for honesty. Time for lateral thinking. Time to create new memories.
Go away together. Stay at home together. Re-create your relationship from
the bottom up. Pretend you're dating again. Be patient. If that doesn't
work, seek professional counselling.*

## 20

# What's your LQ score?

**Imagine you're in the Mastermind chair and your specialist subject is your lover. What would be your love quotient (LQ) score?**

It's a weird one. Ten years into our relationship and we know more about what lights the candle of the person sitting next to us at work than the person we've chosen to share our lives with.

Years ago I read something in one of John Gray's books that has saved me a lot of grief since. John Gray wrote *Men are from Mars, Women are from Venus*, and the point he made – directed at men – was simple: if your partner adores chocolates and sees them as the eternal proof that you love her, why on earth would you buy her roses? Yet the world is full of guys turning up with bunches of roses and wondering why they get thrown at their head. The moral is simple: if your lover needs chocolates to make them feel loved, give 'em chocolates. It's irrelevant whether you think a bunch of red roses is more romantic. You need to give your partner what they need or you might as well not bother.

Here's an idea for you...

**Feel your partner fails to listen to you? Sit them down and talk to them calmly. Huffing about or giving them the silent treatment are passive-aggressive ways of getting nowhere. You have to spell it out.**

Start looking for the 'roses instead of chocolate' trait and you'll start seeing people everywhere doing loads for their loved ones that's going unnoticed. I was quite stunned to discover that after a 'make or break' fight with my partner, all I had to do to appease him was cook him dinner. For whatever screwed up reasons of his psyche, what makes him feel loved isn't gifts of books, CDs, Thai prostitutes or weekends away – it's me getting my pinny on. And when I was upset with him, that's what he would do for me – cook me dinner. For a long time it got him nowhere, as what works for me when I feel angry is long extended conversations – and jewellery of course. Jesting aside, it wasn't until I read the John Gray book that I got it. Our LQs were low. But now when I need to butter him up I just throw a steak on the grill. And when he's upset me, he grits his teeth and gets prepared to bare his soul.

Broadly speaking, to successfully love the person we're with we need to understand what they need to feel loved. To keep their love we must give them what they need as far as possible. If you're reading this and wondering what this has to do with sex, my answer to you is, 'Duh! Just about everything.' Loads of couples are having indifferent or absolutely no sex, not because they don't spark off each other but because they haven't felt loved by their partner for years. The classic example is the bloke faced with a distraught missus, who will 'do' something practical for her – put up shelves, clean her car, pay the bills – when all she wants is a babysitter booked and a meal out.

When your lover's feeling insecure, stressed or worried, how do you make them feel safe and reassured? Does it work? If not, do you know what would? If yes, why do you withhold it from them? Do you like to play mean just for the hell of it? It might seem to work and it might keep you the 'superior' partner, but the price is high. Your partner won't be able to trust you and that sort of trust is near enough essential to keep sex hot between you when the first thrill has gone.

Would your lover rather have a romantic meal or a wild night out on the town as a prelude to sex? Do you occasionally indulge them, even if you'd rather do something else?

**Getting close physically in a non-sexual way inevitably makes it easier to get closer emotionally. Try IDEA 1, *Stop having sex.***

*Try another idea...*

*'Sex is a conversation carried out by another means.'*
PETER USTINOV

*Defining idea...*

Does your partner feel closer to you when you're laughing together or being upset with you? If the answer's 'upset', do you respond in a way that seems to satisfy them or are they disappointed in you? If the answer's 'laughing', when was the last time you went out of your way to make sure you had a good laugh together?

What's your lover's favourite way of resolving a fight (not necessarily the way you always resolve it)?

These are the kind of questions you have to know the answers to. And your partner, of course, has to know what works for you. Emotionally we have to be given chocolates at least some of the time or we start to shut off from our partner and get tempted by someone who appears to offer Milk Tray on demand. If you're with someone for whom chocolate equals love, all the roses in the world won't fix your relationship or help you get good sex.

How was it for you?

**Q**  **We get along fine without having to analyse each other too closely. Why start?**

*A*  *Great. Hope it lasts. But one of the routes to a dull relationship is losing touch with your partner's inner life. Couples need a common goal or they stagnate. Even if you hate analysing each other (or more likely, one of you hates it and imposes that on the other), at least once yearly shoot the breeze about what you want from the next twelve months. What would you like to experience? Visit? Achieve? Is there anything in common that you can work on together?*

**Q**  **My partner won't share anything. How can I change the situation?**

*A*  *When you're distant, a short cut to getting on better is simply to act as if your relationship is perfect – if your lover never speaks to you, carry on talking to them as if they're the world's greatest listener; if your lover never spontaneously shows affection, carry on hugging. Sounds crazy, but the change from negative to positive somehow seeps through to your partner at least long enough for you to ask them to behave more lovingly and for them to hear what you're saying. Keep asking to share, but if they won't it's counselling for you I'm afraid, or you could just put up with it and find some mates with the emotional depth you crave. I still maintain it'll be hell on your long-term sex life though.*

# Bringing up the rear

**Sorry, terrible pun, but the alternative was 'bottoms up', so think yourself lucky.**

Just twenty years ago, anal sex was shocking and unmentionable, but now you can switch on the telly and hear references to it quite routinely. But even if it wasn't talked about much, rear entry has always been mainstream — it's the original form of birth control.

Many couples try anal sex in the first lust-fuelled months of their relationship and then forget about it. If you've tried it and your attitude is 'Been there, done that, don't know what the fuss is about', then it might be time to revisit it. It can add a definite fillip to your lovemaking.

Here's an idea for you...

It goes without saying that a bath or shower together is always a good idea before any sort of rear action. Clip your nails.

## NO LONGER RISQUÉ, JUST PLAIN RISKY

Since you're reading this book, chances are you are already a 'fluid bonded' couple as Americans say, but if not then you need to practise safe sex. Plus, if you touch the anus with tongue, finger, dildo or vibrator, you don't move forward without giving it a jolly good clean. That isn't me making judgements – it's sheer common sense. Bacteria from the cleanest anus can still produce a fearful vaginal infection.

Violet Blue, a sex trainer, has a good tip if you hate interrupting sex to get safe. Wear some rubber gloves and condoms for anal play before peeling them off for vaginal intercourse.

## WHY DO SO MANY MEN FANTASISE ABOUT DOING IT?

I asked some men and their responses included:

■ 'It makes me feel in control and powerful.'

■ 'She only agrees to it when she's really horny and sometimes I set myself the challenge of getting her so turned on that she wants it.'

■ 'It feels different, tighter. Some of my friends say it doesn't, but it does for me.'

And let's not forget the latent homosexual element either, eh boys?

## BUT WHAT'S IN IT FOR WOMEN?

Embarrassed to ask? Turn to
**IDEA 16, *Think kink*.**

*Try another idea...*

Anal sex for men causes friction against the prostate gland – a wonderful thing I'm told, although I'm not qualified to say. But what about for women? The vulval area responds to stretching and that sense of being filled up is terrific for most women. Anal sex works in the same way. Tongues, fingers, dildos and butt plugs can all drive both sexes wild because they give the contracting orgasmic muscles in the bum something to work against.

### Lubrication

It's only in porn films that saliva and free-flowing love juices provide enough lubrication to really enjoy anal sex. That's not to say it can't be done. Half a pint of tequila taken orally is a pretty good lubrication, too, I find. This brings me to another good point. You don't want to be numb when you're having anal sex – from alcohol or from those lubricants sold in sex shops that contain numbing ingredients under the mistaken impression that it's a good thing not to feel sore. Pain is a sign that your body should desist from what it's doing. Anal sex shouldn't be painful and if it is you need to stop and work out what you're doing wrong.

### Rimming

Lots of nerve endings on the anus means that the tongue put to good use can be almost as enjoyable as receiving oral sex. If it doesn't give you an orgasm, it can tip you right over the edge into one. Most common is to use your tongue held at a point to circle round the anal

*'If everything was coated with a seal of approval, some of the fun would go out of it. Let's get away with something. Degrade me, baby.'*
SALLY TISDALE, American writer

*Defining idea...*

91

opening and penetrate in and out, but start with a loose tongue – big licks along the crack feel great and loosen everyone up. Some people like nibbles along the length working towards the anus. As ever, don't put your tongue anywhere else until you've rinsed your mouth.

**Penetration**

Don't attempt anal penetration until your partner is well and truly revved up and a ton of lubrication has been used. Press your finger against the anus, applying pressure.

Massage the opening and slowly slide your finger in up to the first joint. Stay still. You'll feel the ring of muscles around the anus tighten and relax. Don't move your finger, just let the muscles work. When they relax again, slide your finger in slowly.

For women: men can experiment with a finger in the anus and a thumb in the vagina.

For men: women can stimulate his prostate, but only when he's well and truly aroused. You'll feel it as a nub on the front wall of the anus a couple of inches in. It gets bigger as a man gets older and is often described as being the size of a walnut. It responds to pressure and stroking – don't poke and don't prod. Depending on the man this can be quite firm stroking or rhythmic pressure. Ask him for feedback. Stimulation of the prostate while using your mouth our hand to massage his penis results, apparently, in a dynamic, deep orgasm.

Once you've tried with a finger, the world's your oyster. There's a joke there somewhere, but I don't want to think about it too much. If penetrating with a penis or a dildo, the same applies – gentle, rubbing action, unless your lover tells you different, and slow penetration.

Try
another
idea...

**Q**   **I like anal sex and I'd like to try introducing some toys. Literally. It's safe enough, isn't it?**

*A*   *For my sins I know a lot of doctors and one of the common after-dinner conversations when doctors meet socially is recalling the different objects they've had to extricate from patients' bums in casualty. There's a book to be written here, but you'll be relieved to hear this isn't it. Be careful: never insert anything that isn't smooth, unbreakable and flared at the bottom.*

**Q**   **Such as?**

*A*   *Butt plugs provide a terrific sense of fullness and make contractions during orgasm more intense. Holding a vibrator against the butt plug gives delicious sensations. Those small bullet vibrators are almost sitting up and begging to be stuck up your bum, but caution brothers and sisters: most sex toys are shoddily made. Relying on yanking out a bullet or anything else by the electric wire is likely to leave you holding a bit of wire and with a big problem. Stick to rubbing bullets on the perineum.*

## 22

# Sexual confidence

**What is sexual confidence? And how do you get your hands on some?**

If you're uptight about sex, insecure about your body or just plain worried that you're not very good at it, then building sexual confidence is a prerequisite to enjoying yourself.

What factor most affects your ability to have a brilliant sex life? A great body? A fabulous lover? A bendy body? If you've got all these – bully for you. Even so, without one all-important element, your sex life is still likely to be ho-hum rather than bloody fantastic. You must have sexual confidence.

### WHAT MIGHT WORK

This is where my feminist principles go out of the window. Truth is, if you're feeling lacklustre about your appearance – male or female – it's very unlikely you're having a great sex life. Forget *cherchez la femme*, or *cherchez l'homme* for that matter. I say, *cherchez le diet*. A dramatic weight loss in a long-term partner should always be viewed with terrific suspicion. If your lover loses stones and your love life is less than sparkling, you'd better start improving your bedroom skills because their sexual confidence is going to go sky high and when that happens, thrilling sex is never far away. With or without you.

Here's an idea for you... **Work on feeling more sexual every day. Think of yourself as a powerfully sexual person. Look for opportunities to make life more sensual. Flirt.**

On the other hand, if you've been feeling less like sex, ask yourself whether being 5 kg lighter would make a difference to your libido. If it would, then diet. The most successful diet I've come across in recent years is the South Beach Diet by Dr Arthur Agatston. It's healthy and it works.

And this is where I go the whole nine yards and tear up my ticket as a card-carrying feminist. I would love to write with bravado that if you think having bigger/firmer/smaller boobs would improve your sex life you're frankly bonkers. But I'm not sure. As a child, I smashed my teeth falling off a bike. I had bad veneers fitted to replace them. As I proceeded through my twenties, I became self-conscious about smiling and eventually even about talking, so I had new, more expensive dental work and felt more confident. Have I the right to sneer at those who think fiddling with their body parts will make a difference to their sexual confidence? No. But beware. Your goal is sexual confidence. If it's your partner who wants you to have surgery, you won't gain sexual confidence. And if you've had a boob job already, I very much doubt that having smoother thighs will make the difference. These are distractions, and your relationship with either your partner or yourself is at fault. Spend your money on therapy or a self-esteem course instead.

Finally, if you're a bloke, please don't waste your money on penis-enhancing aids that you see in magazines. I'd like to say to you that women don't worry about size, but I can't as they do. But it would be an unusual woman who chucked a bloke because his penis didn't live up to her previous lover's penis. If your penis is smaller than average – anything less than five inches erect – you'll have to be kinder, smarter, funnier and better in bed than other men. Unfair I know, but life isn't fair.

Some penis pumps will work temporarily. There are apparently two operations that can increase either the girth or the length of the penis that actually work. They also can cause problems, and if the penis-lengthening operation goes wrong, you actually end up with a shorter penis. I jest not.

**Feeling cherished can do wonders for our sexual confidence. For ways to do this for your lover look at IDEA 13, *Coming over all touchy-feely.***

*Try another idea...*

## SO WHAT DOES WORK?

- **Change your perception.** Do what it takes you to feel as attractive as you can. Then start talking yourself up: 'I'm happy', 'I look great', 'I'm gorgeous.' Repeat your affirmations twenty times daily.

- **Look in a mirror.** As we get older or busier, we spend less time looking in the mirror and try to pretend our body just isn't there. A mistake. Buy a full-length mirror. Look at yourself naked. Look at yourself dressed. Spend time preening. Throw out everything that doesn't make you feel great and look brilliant. If that leaves you with three items of clothing, so be it.

- **Spend as much time as you can, naked.** This reacquaints you with your body and puts you in touch with your sexual self.

*'If you're one of those people who can't even look in the mirror naked, you need to get used to it. Maybe you need to start with underwear. Maybe you need to start with a Parka, and work down from there. The point is...you're going to have to get comfortable in your own skin.'*
DR PHIL MCGRAW, writing in *O Magazine*

*Defining idea...*

- **Devote an hour a week to loving your body.** If pampering isn't you, start exercising or go to a massage therapist or reflexologist. Anything that gets you back in touch with that thing you need for sex –your body.

*How was it for you?*

**Q   I need to lose weight, but I just can't. What'll make me succeed?**

A   *If you were thinner, how would you behave? What would you be doing? Exercising, eating healthily, buying nice clothes? OK. How can you start doing that tomorrow? The mistake most would-be slimmers make is to think in abstract rather than concrete terms and be too ambitious. You can start exercising tomorrow, but it's highly unlikely you'll start jogging round the park four days a week, which is probably the unrealistic goal you've set yourself. It's also highly unlikely you're going to give up chocolate and crisps overnight, but you could aim to eat fruit or vegetables at every meal. You could buy yourself one nice item of clothing, even if it's in a bigger size – it will make you feel better about yourself. Build up until you're following the sort of lifestyle that will mean you reach your goals.*

**Q   I find my partner less attractive since he got fat. He keeps saying he'll do something about it, but his attempts last two days max. Am I being unreasonable?**

A   *Your attitude is just the sort that won't help. Research studies have shown that it takes people many attempts to succeed at reaching a weight goal, but if they keep persevering, they'll get there. One of the factors that helps them is the unwavering, non-judgemental support of family. That's you.*

## 23

# What you see...

**The general consensus is that men get turned on more than women by visual stimulation. But is it true?**

Could it be that women, freed up to be more sexual, are just beginning to find out what turns them on visually?

The writer J. K. Collins, who was the agony aunt on the first soft porn magazine aimed at heterosexual women, *For Women*, wrote an interesting book entitled *The Sex We Want*. One of the points she makes is that we know a lot about what men find sexually stimulating, but nothing much about what works for women.

I think this applies to visual stimulation in particular. When they view porn, even crap misogynistic porn, women get sexually aroused in just the same physiological ways as men, i.e. there's a flood of blood to their sexual organs. What would the result be of watching porn aimed at exciting both men and women? My point is that women may be able to use visual stimulation to turn them on just as regularly and efficiently as men use it.

During a research group into young women's sexuality that I led for a publishing house, one of the women in the group confessed that she would turn herself on by

**Check out your local large bookshop's erotica section – they've improved out of all recognition in terms of both quality and quantity in the last couple of years.**

pretending to be a stripper in front of a mirror in her bedroom. She really was a private dancer as she cheerfully admitted she would be too embarrassed to perform a striptease for her boyfriend, but she loved to watch while she gradually dropped her clothes until she was naked.

I was reminded of her when I read this passage from *The Hite Report*, where a woman describes how she masturbates: 'Sometimes I dress in erotic costumes and view myself in the mirror. Usually I smoke a cigarette and sometimes I put on make-up. If there is time, I lubricate my breasts and genitals with oil or cream. I prefer looking in the mirror rather than directly at myself. I begin playing with my breasts...'

Another woman in *The Hite Report* says, 'My best "quickie, one-minute special" is standing up with my vibrator, on my toes, totally tensed...with the vibrator tip against the clitoris and holding the body of the vibrator out, so it looks like a penis – in front of the mirror. I get turned on by my image doing this and come in a minute.'

What's interesting is that all these women observe themselves. Is that for want of any other material? My theory is that once women get used to the idea of getting turned on visually, they will. As J. K. Collins points out in her book, the failure of sex magazines aimed at women (including *For Women*) could have something to do with the fact that they can't show erect dicks. (When you think about what's out there now, how ridiculous is that?) Still, women might find that gay magazines aimed at either sex work for you. Or it could be the sight of restraints on your lover. Or dressing him as a gladiator. Actively look for images that turn you on and use them in fantasy and lovemaking to make you feel more sexually vibrant. The reason I think this is worth going on about is that it's one of the easiest and quickest ways to keep your libido alive and kicking, and we need as much of that as we can in a long-term relationship.

Turn to IDEA 48, *See things differently*, for other ways of exploring visual stimulation.

*Try another idea...*

Wear clothes to bed that turn you on. If you love the way your breasts look in a push-up bra, keep it on. I know one woman who wore a favourite pair of red stilettoes to bed. They did nothing for her bloke, but she used to lie with her feet in the air, admiring what those shoes did for the length of her legs. Love yourself!

This is all easier for women as the sexual female body is a ubiquitous image (and why women find it easy to observe themselves for titillation), but men don't often get the chance to be sex objects. So why not be different? If you really want to rock her world, hire a fireman's outfit for the night. I have no idea why, but it would be a rare women, who wouldn't appreciate the gesture.

Use mirrors – line them up so you can see yourself from all angles. Then experiment with lighting. A torch adds a creepy, otherworldly quality to proceedings and you might find that interesting. It's also hard to get the image of shagging by candlelight out of your mind afterwards, which is a bit less scary and a lot more flattering than a camcorder. Though of course, that works on the same principle.

*'Sexual intercourse is kicking death in the ass while singing.'*
CHARLES BUKOWSKI, writer

*Defining idea...*

**How was it for you?**

**Q    Books, films, etc., don't do a thing for me. What's my next move?**

A    *OK. But remember it's just conditioning that tells men that suspenders and stockings are sexy. A friend of mine spent months mincing around the bedroom in various versions of the full tackle, with no significant effect on her boyfriend. She finally asked him what turned him on (radical idea, I know) and he answered, 'One of those neck to floor white cotton nightdresses like your granny might wear, with buttons up the front.' Who would have ever guessed? You may have to be sexual commandos, fearlessly tracking down new territory before you find what turns each other on.*

**Q    Any suggestions for women-friendly visual aids?**

A    *Try the web: www.nerve.com has a photo gallery, or there's the bookshop at www.gash.co.uk. You could also try making your own porn movie (turning the camcorder on you and your lover, I hasten to add). Reliving some of your greatest moments before you get it on should spur you onto greater heights.*

# 24

# Blow jobs 101

**Put a little thought into your next blow job – he'll appreciate it.**

Boy meets girl. Girl meets boy. Love and mutual respect blossoms. And before long the question of fellatio raises its occasionally ugly head.

Of course you know how to do this. Perhaps it was one of the first things you learned. But maybe a little refresher is in order (and I don't just mean a mouthwash).

## THE BASIC MENU

Whatever your technique, it's worth making sure it includes these moves:

■ Use your tongue to circle around the rim on the head of the penis quite firmly and to run up and down the ridge on the underside until it meets the small piece of skin where the head meets the shaft – the frenulum. Doing this stimulates two of the most sensitive parts of the penis (if he's uncircumcised – but try it even if he is).

Here's an idea for you...

**Ask him to run his hands through your hair or touch the side of your face while you're going down on him. Men don't often think to do this, and women don't ask them because for most women the sense of having their head controlled is an unpleasant one, but there's a world of difference between a man keeping contact by gently ruffling your hair and gripping your ears in a death grip.**

Defining idea...

*'Oral sex is currently very trendy. It is even preferred to the regular kind. It is preferred because it's the only way most of us can get our partners to shut up.'*
P. J. O'ROURKE

■ Massage the perineum (the spot between the testicles and anus) while you're going down – a vibrator is good for this.

■ After years together, you may be taking his pleasure somewhat for granted. For most men, the easiest way to make them think they're getting a great blow job is for you to seem to be having a fine time. So, give it all the enthusiasm you would the finest chocolate ice-cream and if the odd moan of pleasure escapes all the better. Or you could hum – some women swear by humming while they're giving oral sex, as the vibrations heighten the sensation on the penis.

**EXTRAS**

Add sensations that make him even more aware of what's going on down there.

1. Swirl mouthwash around your mouth before going down: the mint tingles and makes him more tuned into the heat of your mouth. Toothpaste gives an even more extreme sensation.

2. Bite into a lemon.

3. Hold a mouthful of neat vodka in your mouth as long as you can. Try this tentatively at first. Sensitive souls feel it as a burn.

4. Hot tea (not boiling) used the same way can engulf him in a warm bath of sensation.

5. An ice cube crushed in your mouth will be excruciatingly sensitive. Or keep the ice cube intact and work it around his penis as you move your mouth up and down.

6. If you're really coordinated, try hot and cold in succession. This can be a bit of a feat, so to keep him in sexual wonderland and retain your mystique it helps to blindfold him first, kiss him generously all over, fool him that that's the main course and then make with the hot/cold routine. Done teasingly this can be great fun for both of you.

**Turn to IDEA 33, *More on blow jobs*, for more ideas on giving him oral sex.**

*Try another idea...*

'Fellating is fun, but it's hard work. After twenty minutes it's just hard work.'
EM and LO, sex agony aunts on nerve.com

*Defining idea...*

105

How was
it for
you?

**Q**   I've tried your tips, but my partner is pretty silent and I don't
know if he's embarrassed by the moves or enjoying them. How can
I find out?

**A**   *You need to make it clear in a charming way to your partner that staying
silent when receiving oral sex isn't helpful. Appreciative groans are the very
least that a lover should expect. It's good manners and it spurs you on to
greater efforts. But better than mutterings is clear direction. We are
probably more individualistic in the way we prefer to receive oral sex than
anything else in the sexual repertoire. One woman I interviewed told me
that her husband preferred her to use her teeth – hard – when she was
going down on him. Now this is unusual, and my point is not to start
gnawing on your lover's manhood (although some men may well enjoy a
light grazing). My point is that you don't know what he likes unless he tells
you. Even if it's a longstanding partner, ask. Take the pressure off them by
making it non-judgemental on your performance. It helps to say, 'Do you
like this (demonstration) better than this (further demonstration)?' Most
times the response will be 'Whatever, just don't stop.' But occasionally you'll
learn something useful.*

**Q**   It takes ages for me to come. What's the best route to home base?

**A**   *Give her a break and change the rhythm – use your hand or encourage her
to swap to penetration or hand jobs. If she's just not giving you the right
stimulation, vary your technique. Do you find it hard to relax and enjoy oral
sex? This is common in women and there's no reason why men should
escape. Women do like fellating and can really get off on it. Talk to your
lover and perhaps use fantasy to overcome an inability to relax.*

# 25

# Dressing up and staying in

**Acting out fantasies takes a bit of practice, but can certainly brighten up a boring Saturday night.**

First get into bed and talk dirty to one another. Read from some mildly pornographic books (or filthy pornographic books, if you like). Share some situations that turn you on mentally. Talk through the sorts of things you'd like to say or do

The next obvious step is to pick a night to play out your fantasy, although sometimes it's best just to go for it spontaneously as it helps you to feel less self-conscious. Even if the first time is a disaster and lasts about two minutes before you start laughing, at least you've made a start.

You won't have to expend any money on special outfits unless you want to, as you can improvise with dressing up and props. Again, it helps if one of you (the one who will be dominant in the fantasy makes the most sense) takes control of organising and briefing the other on their role.

*Here's an idea for you...*

**Crack open a bottle (or two). As with all fantasy games, alcohol helps loosen you up. A lot.**

Some people find costumes liberating and that they help them get into character. Some people find them inhibiting, not to say ridiculous. But don't give up too early on them because they can help. Before you know it, you'll be down the local fancy-dress shop for your Robin Hood or nun's outfit.

## SIX CLICHÉD (AND-THAT'S-BECAUSE-THEY-WORK) FANTASY ROLE-PLAYS

### Doctor and nurse

It's the end of another gruelling day on the wards. The nurse (either one of you) is looking exhausted. The doctor calls the nurse over and says, 'You're looking tired. Could you do with a complete examination?' The doctor gets the examination table ready and asks the nurse to lie down on it. A complete medical later and the diagnosis is 'nervous tension'. However, the doctor is conducting a scientific study into this condition, with some controversial treatment options. If the nurse is willing to take part in some medical experimentation and give feedback on how well the cure works, the doctor will demonstrate the technique...

### Master and slave

One of you is the cruel master (or mistress); one is the gorgeous slave. The master is deciding whether to buy or not, which involves a thorough examination. The slave is wrapped in layers of clothes and drapes but is slowly stripped (or ordered to strip) so the master can confirm that the slave is in good physical condition – and that means that every bit of them is in good physical condition. Then, of course, the slave's ability to follow orders and please the master will have to be tested....

## Boss and interviewee

The interviewee comes to the office after hours to be interviewed for their dream job. The interview starts normally: the interviewee is anxious to please and the interviewer is gracious. However, when they start discussing terms of employment, some of the terms are quite unusual. Late-night working? Threesomes with the head of personnel and the boss? Finally, there is an initiative test – how well the interviewee performs determines whether they get the job....

**IDEA 50, *Dream time*, has more on fantasy.**

*Try another idea...*

## Husband and the Swedish au pair

He is the innocent, she the fun-loving au pair (extra points if she can keep the accent going all the way through). The wife is away and he's settling down to watch the football when she asks if she can join him. Is he seeing things or is her skirt always that short? And is she sitting a little closer than normal? She seems more flirtatious, more brazen. Double meanings and loaded looks are passing between them. He tries to get a grip of himself and resist temptation while she goes out of her way to seduce him into making the first move. Until finally, losing patience, she makes her intentions quite clear....

*'It would be rude to get your sexual satisfaction by tying someone to the bed and then leaving him or her there and going out with someone more attractive.'*
P. J. O'ROURKE

*Defining idea...*

### Handy man and housewife

He arrives ready for work, but she insists he has a cup of tea and a chat. While she's showing him the problem 'with her pipes', she gets into such a position that he can't help noticing she's not wearing any underwear....

### Naughty maid and 'master of the house'

She's supposed to be cleaning the house when the 'master' comes home and discovers her 'pleasuring' herself instead. He's furious and threatens her with dismissal. She is beside herself. She'll lose her job. She has to think of something quick that will persuade him that sacking her is a bad idea....

**Q** **I think about acting out fantasies, but I feel too self-conscious. How can I get over this?**

*How was it for you?*

*A* *Acting out a role that's already predetermined removes performance pressure, so copy some scenes from movies. You'll then have a rough dialogue already – what you can remember from the script. For instance, anyone can do a duff Scottish accent and an unbelievable Eastern European one, so every couple can play James Bond and Bond Girl. If you can persuade him to wear a DJ, even better. A couple I know of used to 'be' Jessica Lange and Jack Nicholson in* The Postman Always Rings Twice. *It was their shorthand for wild out-of-control sex and whenever she fancied some, he'd come home to find her roaming about their kitchen sporting low cleavage, tight skirt, extremely high heels and a drawl like Blanche Dubois on a pint of bourbon. In his words, 'I fancied her so much, I couldn't walk straight.' After a bit of flirting, he'd throw her on the kitchen table and rip her clothes off.*

**Q** **Our home doesn't lend itself to acting out fantasies. How can we set the scene?**

*A* *Lighting helps. Make sure that you have low-key lighting, whether from candles, a pin torch or a low lamp – whatever is appropriate for the fantasy. But please, this doesn't have to be an Oscar-winning production. The main thing is to get rid of any clutter – especially the kids' toys and any photos of your mother. The only essential in terms of location is to get rid of anything that even the world's most active imagination would balk at finding sexy.*

111

# 26

# Handy work

**What they never taught you at art class...**

Bringing your partner off with your hand is a staple of a good sex life and for men an essential skill to develop as this is the only way most women can come during intercourse.

We get into habits with achieving orgasm, just like everything else. We are welded to one way of stimulating ourselves to climax and then (if we're lucky) our partners get proficient at mimicking us and that's the sort of stimulation we get from them. Terrific. No one's knocking that, but ringing the changes and using a different technique can teach you a lot about your sexual response and can result in deeper orgasms. It starts off as a frustrating process – it takes a while to retrain yourself – but rely on the Tantric principle, 'It's the journey not the arrival that's important.' Doing this will make you closer as a couple and it will make you more orgasmic.

Experiment with the following techniques when you're masturbating – once you've got the hang of them, share your new knowledge with your partner. Remember, if you're the one doing the stimulating, don't chop and change between techniques too much in one session, as it's distracting, especially when your partner's approaching orgasm.

**Lots of manual work can lead to chafing, so lubricate, lubricate, lubricate. Then lubricate some more.**

## DIFFERENT FOR GIRLS

■ Make a fist, place it on the top of the vulva and move it from there. Experiment with position and pressure until you find what works best. Careful, because it's easy to ruin the mood by being too enthusiastic – this one needs lots of communication.

■ After rubbing the clitoral area with fingers, moving onto a palm provides an intense pressure and an intense orgasm. Using the heel of the palm to grind against the clitoris while the fingers are free to play around with the vagina, perineum and labia gives strong contractions, especially if you press down just above the pubic bone at the same time with your other hand. If you're doing this to your partner, it works well in positions where they are free to grind against the heel of your palm.

■ The wishbone, sometimes known as 'the V', uses the whole of the clitoris and not just the little nub that we call the clitoris – that's just the bit we see. Spreading outwards and downwards from the clitoris nub, on either side of the vagina and under the skin are the arms of the clitoris. Place your index and middle fingers pointed downwards towards the vagina, one on each side of the labia with the junction of the V on your clitoris nub. Massage the clitoral arms and the clitoris with the V, keeping up constant pressure on all parts of the clitoris. The orgasm from this technique takes time, but that builds tension and gives most women a more diffuse orgasm that's more of a whole body experience. Partners can use this during rear-entry positions by reaching round your waist.

■ Insert the index finger of one hand into the vagina and pull down very gently (if you're masturbating, reaching from behind with your hand might be easier). With the other finger rub up and down on the clitoral hood. The stretching will feel great.

**Women: for explosive orgasms combine manual work with IDEA 29, *Easy routes to faster orgasm for her.***

Try another idea...

## MEN ONLY

■ After some preliminary strokes to get things hotted up, hold the penis with one hand and place the palm of the other hand across the head. For every up movement and down movement, circle the other hand over the head. As one hand comes up you circle over. As the hand goes down you circle again. The hands come close together on the up stroke. Get into a rhythm.

■ Clasp both hands around the penis with fingers interlaced and move up and down.

■ Make your hands into two 'beaks'. Use one starting at the base of the penis and move up and another around the balls and pull them slightly outwards at the same time. Relax. Repeat. This takes practice and isn't enough to bring most men off, but it's terrific for men who like their balls played with.

*'I don't say anything during sex. I've been told not to. Told during sex, in fact.'*
CHEVY CHASE

Defining idea...

- Here's one to practise as he's approaching orgasm. Clasp both hands around the head of his penis and squeeze, hold for a second, let go and squeeze again. You're trying to mimic the rhythm of his pulse and it can heighten the orgasm if done while he's ejaculating.

How was it for you?

**Q  My partner says I'm too rough. Have you got any guidelines?**

A  *Men: if you're not sure about how much pressure to apply and what rhythm to adopt when you're bringing a woman off with your hand, the general advice is to go half as hard and twice as slow as you think will work. Get feedback from your partner. Encourage her to let you know when she wants it done differently. As with oral sex, if she's bucking against your hand that's a good indication that she likes what you're doing and wants harder, faster stimulation.*

**Q  I come when I masturbate, but not when my husband uses his hand, even though he's doing it right. What's wrong?**

A  *It could be that you have a mental block with this for some reason. Use fantasy to get over it. You're taking part in a medical experiment – the results will save humankind. You're a goddess and your high priest's greatest pleasure is servicing you. Orgasm is a mind game so cheat your brain.*

## 27

# Heading south

**Enjoy the journey and she'll be ecstatic.**

It's been said that if you think of the clitoris as being the centre of a clock, most women get the most pleasure at 10 to 2. Want to know more? Then read on.

'When a lover goes down on me, anything can happen. From the first silky caress of a warm tongue on my clitoris to the crashing moment of orgasm as a hot mouth envelopes my vulva, I have the possibilities of the world between my legs. I can be anyone, anywhere: a woman arrested for speeding, bent over the hood of her car...I can role play with my lover as a ravished femme, a dominant mistress, or a naughty schoolgirl. I can be the one woman my partner desires the most, with their face deliciously pressed between my legs in an act of worship that I can enjoy as either sacred or profane. But whenever, however, wherever it happens, I know I'm going to have a sexual experience that is at once tender and intimate, one that results in a powerful, focused orgasm.'

That's how Violet Blue, a sex instructor, starts her book *The Ultimate Guide to Cunnilingus*, and I quote it in full because it reminds us why going down is tops. It guarantees an orgasm for more women, more of the time. Women who find it difficult to come find it easy this way.

Here's an idea for you... **This one comes from Violet Blue's *Ultimate Guide to Cunnilingus*. Make a diamond with your hands and lay this over the labia to hold the 'lips' apart to give you full access. Leaning against the bridge made by your fingers also gives you support when you need it.**

*Defining idea...* **'Porn is a lousy place to learn how to perform oral sex on a woman: most on-screen cunnilingus looks like an exaggerated version of Fido with a mouthful of peanut butter. However, adult instructional videos can be very helpful.'**
VIOLET BLUE, sex instructor

## POSITIONS

Three things are essential:

1.  The woman should be able to relax and not worry about supporting herself, such as lying back on the bed or sitting on the edge of a table.

2.  The man should be comfortable – he might be there for a while. If you're on a bed, then support her bum on a couple of pillows. Or she could lie with her legs over the edge of the bed and he can kneel on the floor. Or do a variation of this on any table, chair, worktop, etc.

3.  Some couples enjoy the classic subservient oral sex pose. Men, you're the subservient one – on your knees while she stands in front of you. But this can make access difficult for you, and orgasm difficult for her. It's a bit easier if she supports one leg on a chair or low table, but the biggest thrill from this one tends to be the dominatrix element not the position.

NB Men: 69s are fun and so is the traditional 'sitting on the face' position. These look great visually – which is why they're so popular in porn films – as well as being exciting and/or relaxing for you. But just so you know, although women can get deeply excited during these positions, few women will go over the edge and come. That's because women tend to have to be able to relax and concentrate in the build up to their orgasm. Muck about with different positions as much as you like as part of 'foreplay' – she'll enjoy it – but when you're serious about giving your woman an orgasm, don't expect any more of her than lying back and luxuriating in what you're doing to her.

**Read more on cunnilingus in IDEA 32, *Heading even further south.***

*Try another idea…*

## TWO GOOD TO GO AT ANY TIME

Take your time. Start wherever you like and suck, kiss, nibble, apply hard pressure, apply short pressure, or blow (but never into the vagina, as there's a million to one chance you could give her an embolism). Work towards the clitoris, work around the sides of it, but don't touch it until her hips are writhing towards you and she's practically grabbing your ears for direction. Use a big wide lick, like you were eating an ice-cream. Get a lot of lubrication down there and many women will enjoy lapping more than more direct pointy-tongue action.

Remember that for lots of women the clitoris is too sensitive to take too much direct action, and that's why the big lick works so well.

How was it for you?

**Q** **My wife never seems enthusiastic about cunnilingus. How can I persuade her?**

*A* *Usually I'd say not to push something that your wife doesn't seem to like, but oral sex is tied up with so many body issues and 'shame' thoughts that loads of women just can't lie back and enjoy it – they need to be trained to believe that it's really OK. If you seem reluctant to go down on your missus, she may be less than keen. Having a man get up close and personal makes women feel very vulnerable. And quite right too. It would be a total waste of time as if a woman's tense and anxious, there's absolutely no chance of her coming, so why would she (or you) bother? She may be worrying that she'll take ages to come. Reassure her that you don't care. If she comes, terrific. If she doesn't, no big deal. If I were you I wouldn't keep going for ages, not because you're a selfish lover, but because she won't feel the performance pressure to come if you make it clear it's part of your foreplay. Go down on her often so she gets the idea that you like it and there's no pressure on her. With time, she might relax enough to start enjoying it.*

**Q** **I don't like giving head. Why should I?**

*A* *Well, if your partner's enjoying terrific orgasms and doesn't care – fine. But this really is a marvellous treat for most women and to deprive your partner of it is a shame. I take it for granted that there are no issues of hygiene here that should be addressed first. Remember that a significant number of women can only come this way and that the sensation is unique – when a tongue makes you come, you know it. Women feel so chuffed with the person who gave them an orgasm through oral sex that it's well worth persevering from your point of view, too. You'll gain shedloads of brownie points.*

# Short cuts to better orgasms

**We're coming over all PC**

*Orgasm depends on the rhythmic contraction of muscles. Train these muscles and you're going to have better orgasms.*

If you're a woman, especially one who's had children, you'll be tired of discussions about your pubococcygeal (PC) muscles. These are the muscles that take a lot of the strain when you're pregnant and in labour, and so midwives and doctors stress the importance of exercising them every chance you get because without your PC muscles, to put it bluntly, you'll need nappies for longer than the baby. Hats off to Dr Arnold Kegel, the man who first recommended these exercises to help bladder control following childbirth. But I can't help thinking that if doctors were to stress how much 'doing Kegels' can improve your love life (for both sexes), then a lot more of us would be doing them.

Tensing and releasing these muscles increases blood flow to the genitals – and when you focus benign interest on your genitals, it tends to improve your sex life. But there's more. These are the muscles that contract during orgasm. The stronger they are, the better the contraction and the more pleasure you feel.

Here's an idea for you... **Need motivation to do your Kegels? You should notice improvements within two weeks. And within six weeks, you should feel the difference in your love life. So get clenching.**

For men, strengthening your PC muscles may help you experience multiple orgasms. By having strong PC muscles you can stop on the brink of ejaculating and experience orgasm without actually coming, so you can continue to make love for longer. Exercising your PC muscles will give you better orgasms, and this is A Good Thing for men whose orgasm often seems to be less encompassing than their partner's orgasm.

## FINDING YOUR PC MUSCLES

Next time you pee, stop the stream of urine mid-flow. The muscles that you're using to do that are the PC muscles. Make sure that you isolate them from the muscles surrounding the anus.

## YOUR EXERCISE PROGRAMME

Simply contract your PC muscles every time you remember – ten times for a couple of seconds each time. Don't overdo it and don't squeeze too hard. Aim for a steady, relaxed contraction.

Once you've got the hang of that, ring the changes and contract twelve times at normal speed and twelve times at a faster speed. Do this twice a day – more if you remember – for the rest of your life. And if you're really dedicated, aim for 100 Kegels a day.

## FOR ADVANCED EXERCISERS

On top of your standard Kegels, try these:

■ **The lift.** Imagine that your vagina has a lift inside it and you're going to elevate the lift using your PC muscles. Take the lift to the first floor, pause, second floor, pause, third floor, pause, top floor, pause. Now let the lift down again. Practice and practice this, going as fast as possible and then as slowly as possible.

■ **Pelvic tilts.** Combine your Kegels with pelvic tilts, which strengthen your back and pelvis muscles so you can thrust better and for longer. Lie on the floor with your knees bent and feet flat on the floor. Contract your stomach and tilt your pelvis up, keeping your spine on the floor. Contract your PCs as you do this, hold for a couple of seconds and then return to the beginning position. Do up to twenty tilts day.

**During sex, combine Kegel action with techniques in IDEA 29, *Easy routes to faster orgasm for her.***

*Try another idea...*

**'It is easier to keep half a dozen lovers guessing than to keep one lover after he has stopped guessing.'**
HELEN ROWLAND, American journalist

*Defining idea...*

123

*How was it for you?*

**Q** **These exercises aren't enough. Since my kids, I can barely feel a twitch when I contract my PCs. What else can I do?**

A *Your orgasms probably feel much weaker, too. But you can get the strength back. It's probably worth making it more of a project and setting aside a particular time each day to do your Kegels. Remember that it's not just your sex life that will benefit. After the menopause when hormonal changes make your PC muscles even weaker, you'll be grateful you took action now. You'll find it easier with something to hold on to when doing the above exercises, such as a finger, dildo or carrot. Or you could be a trifle more scientific and invest in some weighted barbells – you can buy these in chemists and over the internet (try www.gash.co.uk for the Energie Kegel Exerciser). You'll then get an indication of how weak your muscles are now and you'll be able to measure your progress as you improve. And you will.*

**Q** **So exactly how do strong PCs stop me ejaculating?**

A *When you feel your PCs are strengthened, while you're masturbating try to contract them at the point just before orgasm. This stops you ejaculating, but you should still feel pleasure. The point is you should be able to get going again after a short break. When you read up about this, it can sound a bit like a competitive sport – lots of macho bragging about never coming, being a 'master of control', etc. That kind of thing worries me. But time spent learning more about your sexual response is never wasted, plus you may want to experience a multiple orgasm – who wouldn't? But it's not necessarily going to make you a better lover. Just so you know, Eastern bods recommend that men only come maybe once every three times they have sex. But that once is stronger, better and more thrilling, or so they say.*

# 29

# Easy routes to faster orgasm for her

**Quicker, harder, faster? How to come more easily.**

Tweaking your usual lovemaking pattern can improve your sex life with a minimal amount of effort. We could have called this chapter 'How to have a simultaneous orgasm', but we've always thought that an overrated pastime. However, if you insist....

### SQUEEZING

When you orgasm, your pubococcygeal (PC) muscles in the vagina contract rapidly. Tighten your PC muscles as he withdraws, and relax them as he enters. It'll take a bit of practice but this is a recommendation from the queen of the female orgasm, Betty Dodson, who through her workshops and books has taught thousands of women how to come, and how to come better. Squeezing will jump-start your own orgasmic contractions.

Here's an idea for you... **To increase your chances of simultaneous orgasm, let your partner know how excited you are and encourage the same feedback from him. If you want to minimise prosaic chat, whisper a number to your mate to let him know exactly where on a scale of 1 to 10 you are in terms of getting your rocks off. He can do the same.**

## PRESSING

Downward pressure on your pubic area before orgasm can increase the intensity of stimulation. Experiment with pressing down with your hand on your stomach just above your pubic bone while masturbating or using a vibrator. Then try this during intercourse. Another technique is to 'bear down'. This is pushing out with your PC muscles, which may help force your G-spot closer to your vaginal opening so it's likelier to get indirect stimulation from his penis.

## STRETCHING

Stretching your legs flat on the bed and bringing them together while in the missionary position will increase clitoral stimulation. It works even better when you're on top. Slide your thighs down so they are over his thighs rather than his hips. Arch your back so you're bending backwards. Forming an arc means you'll be putting maximum pressure on the clitoral area. Just be careful you don't bend his penis back too far – you have all the control here and being a gent he might not want to interrupt your obvious pleasure to tell you that you're in imminent danger of breaking it off.

It's also worth experimenting with other positions where you are on top and your feet are stretched down towards his feet. These tend to increase clitoral stimulation.

## HANGING

Hang your head over the edge of the bed when you're having sex. The rush of blood to the brain increases sensations.

**Check out the CAT position in IDEA 5, *Join the 30%*. It encourages clitoral stimulation.**

*Try another idea...*

'**Failing to give each other some basic direction can leave couples guessing – and frustrated. Not a big talker in bed? These four words should get you by just fine: "faster", "slower", "harder" and "softer".'**
JUDY DUTTON, writing in *She* magazine

*Defining idea...*

**How was it for you?**

**Q How can we attain synchronicity? Whatever we do, I take ages to come. Unless he brings me off first, he always comes first.**

A *Hey, don't knock it! Try a vibrator. It's the easiest way to synchronise orgasms. But if you aren't happy with this or want to ring the changes, you could try some mind tricks. The first is to free yourself of performance pressure – fixating on having an orgasm is the surest way to stop yourself having one. The minute the thought 'God, it's taking ages' enters your mind, immediately switch off and begin to live in the moment. Come back to your body, concentrate on the sensations and focus on your pleasure.*

**Q Why does it take women so much longer?**

A *It doesn't. It's been estimated that through intercourse it takes men 11 minutes to come and women 28 minutes. (How do they know this stuff?) But let's get one thing straight. When it comes to masturbation, women come as quickly as men. So why do women take longer to come during intercourse? My theory is that men are more revved up mentally beforehand than women. A woman's orgasm will happen more quickly if you feel sexier before the action begins. After folding the ironing, don't expect to be howling orgasmically five minutes later. While your bloke is still watching the news, start warming yourself up. Create your own 20-minute ritual for separating your working day from your time with your partner. Have a shower or bath with sweet-smelling products, light candles, wear sensuous nightwear or read a sexy story. This can make an immense difference to how quickly you orgasm.*

# 30

# Assume the position...

**...but ring the changes**

We promised no line drawings of beardie-weirdie men doing the sort of things that beardie-weirdie men love to do. And we're going to keep our promise.

Books of positions have always struck me as appealing predominantly to the anoraks among us who want a definitive list of every position ever known and a nice sharp pencil with which to tick them off. What is generally not known is that the *Kamasutra* was written with the élite of (male) Indian society in mind who had nothing else to do all day but think of ways of pleasuring their personal harem. Working your way through the *Kamasutra* ain't going to cut it with your average dual-income, too-busy-to-breathe couple. As we non-anoraks know, it's going to take more than a swift bout of 'bending the rushes' to keep our love life exciting.

There are basically only four or five positions (no, I can't be arsed to count them), and everything else is just a variation on a theme. However, most couples find one or two favourites and stick with these because they deliver. Some simple

Here's an idea for you... **The simplest, but very effective modification of the missionary position is an ancient Eastern technique: she stuffs a couple of pillows under her hips to raise her pelvis, which improves clitoral stimulation.**

modifications can make these even better. Here is a summary and some more ideas on improving on a good thing.

## THREE WAYS TO MAKE A GOOD THING BETTER

### Improve...the missionary

A great position, much maligned. There are two potential problems:

1. Most women won't come this way, even if he pumps away for three hours. Not unless some clitoral stimulation is brought into play.

2. He has to work harder – a lot harder.

So here's an alternative for when you both want to be on the bottom. She lies with her left leg flat on the bed and the right one bent at the knee and can lean on her elbows or prop herself up with cushions. He lies at right angles to her on his left side, supporting himself on his left arm while his lower (left leg) passes under her left thigh so he lifts up her pelvis enough to enter. She hooks her right leg over his ribcage. This should form a sort of open-scissors arrangement, which allows free access for both parties to her clitoris and means you can both gaze soulfully into each other's eyes even if you're too far away for a kiss. Movement is limited, but this is a good position for when you're feeling lazy – great for when you both have a hangover.

## Improve...Her on top

Very popular position with women. Very popular with men for that matter. Here's something to try:

She gets on top and squats on top of him then gently swivels round so that she's facing his feet. She may have to bend forward a bit and use his ankles or calves to hold on to. He gets a superlative view of her bottom as opposed to her breasts. Also, if she lifts herself up between thrusts, he gets a great view of his penis entering her – probably the closest view you can get of penetration, short of a porn movie. Perhaps that's the reason this position was voted the one most men would like to try in a *Cosmopolitan* survey. And if she wriggles about, she'll get good stimulation of the area around her G-spot, plus few positions will give her so much scope to fantasise.

**I could be being a little bit dismissive of the power of changing positions – a book stuffed full of exotic ways to do it combined with IDEA 17, *Learn the art of kaizen*, could work a treat for you.**

*Try another idea...*

## Improve...The 69

Great fun in theory, but as orgasm approaches it gets harder to concentrate on giving pleasure. One partner loses concentration, and bang, the show's over for the other one, which is one reason why couples tend to stop doing 69s once their honeymoon period is over. Remember, it's easier if you lie on your side leaning on the inside of your lover's thigh for support. You can also pass a vibrator between you so that if one of you is approaching orgasm, he or she can stop tongue action and stimulate with the vibrator instead so that your lover stays revved up while bringing you off.

*'I once had a rose named after me and I was very flattered. But I was not pleased to read the description in the catalogue: no good in a bed, but fine up against a wall.'*
ELEANOR ROOSEVELT

*Defining idea...*

*How was it for you?*

**Q** **I like standing positions, but since my husband did his back in, I've been scared to suggest any. Any ideas?**

*A* *You could wear a pair of really high heels and lean against a wall. He'll barely have to move. They look great, too. (If you brace your hands against the wall for support, the position is sometimes called the 'strip search' for obvious reasons – I'll leave it to your imagination to work out how role-play could be brought into play here). Rear entry in general is helpful for standing positions. The easiest way is for you to bend forward and support yourself on the floor or a low table or chair. You have to be pretty supple and, for whatever reason, this is easier to accomplish in the bath with you using the sides of the bath for support. Just be careful not to slip or you'll have more than your back to worry about.*

**Q** **In some positions, I feel pain when my partner enters me. Why is this?**

*A* *He could be hitting against your cervix. General rule: the nearer your feet are to your ears, the deeper the penetration. Rear-entry positions also usually allow deep penetration (which is why they're favoured by our less well-endowed brothers). By lowering your thighs during missionary-type positions, you'll be able to control the depth of his thrusting. Similarly, if you like doing rear entry, try spoon positions where you both lie side to side with him behind you – again, you'll be controlling the level of thrust. It goes without saying that if pain during sex continues it should be reported to your doctor.*

# 31

# Bunty and Daisy rather than Sadie and Maisie

**Or for those of you who prefer acronyms – soft-core B&D (bondage and discipline) rather than hard-core S&M (sadism and masochism).**

If your average Saturday night involves being spanked on a stage in front of strangers, skip over this as I'm not going to bring anything new to your party. This chapter is aimed at people who've never really tried B&D.

**WHAT'S THE POINT?**

What I love about hard-core health spas – the ones where you get timetables and set menus involving lots of lentils – is that you don't have to think. You just do what you're told. That's what the submissive partner gets in B&D games. In forgoing all control, there's a whole heap of freedom.

Here's an idea for you...

**For those of you who still aren't convinced about the whole B&D thing, check out a trilogy of fantasy books by Jaqueline Carey – *Kushiel's Dart* and its sequels. They're not 'top shelf' in any way, but the heroine is a very unsubmissive masochist and the books are erotic without being porno. They might make you keener to experiment and give you some ideas.**

As for the dominant partner – what's not to love? They get to do exactly what they want, exactly the way they like it. Perfect for anal compulsives, who most of the time can't get the rest of us to do it their way. On our knees, on our back, tied up, tied down or licking the heel of your shoes for twenty minutes. It's your call.

The pain you experience in these sorts of games isn't pain like when you catch your finger in the door. When pain is anticipated, it raises your heart rate and releases the feel-good hormones endorphins – just what happens during exercise. One effect of this is that you can experience heightened sexual pleasure and sensation. When things get painful, try deep steady breathing, which makes sexual sensations even stronger.

It goes without saying that all of this goes down well with a bit of role-play. Modify some of the scenarios in this book, or make up your own. It's your night to shine. Or to be hogtied and locked in a cupboard, if that's what lights your candle.

When playing with power games that involve humiliation and control there's always the chance you'll hurt another person, and I don't mean just physically. You should both agree on a word beforehand that immediately signals 'game's over, time for lots of cuddling and reassurance'. That word shouldn't be 'no' as then you wouldn't be able to scream 'please stop, oh no, you bastard' thus losing out on half the fun. It's an absolute rule that if either of you utter 'the word', then you stop.

## POWER GAMES

1. **Tying up.** Play with exposure (generally, the wider the limbs are spread, the more you feel like you're open to the public – some people like that). Restraints on all four limbs are great for people who find it hard to come because of performance pressure to 'get there'. Restraint puts you totally at the mercy of your partner. You are in their power. They have responsibility. You can relax. Whoosh. Was that an orgasm?

2. **Spanking.** Always warm up the spankee's buttocks beforehand with some gentle slaps and then build up in a rhythmic way with gaps between strokes. The back of a hairbrush or a table tennis bat make good alternatives if your hand is getting sore. As a general rule, never hit any part of the body that is hard. In fact, don't hit anything but the buttocks unless you know what you're doing. After administering a whupping and when the skin is still pink and tingly, run your fingers gently over their skin. This will feel exquisite.

3. **Gags.** This is more a mind thing than anything else. It looks great and it makes you feel really helpless – loads of opportunity to flail your head from side to side in best teen-slasher movie style. Tongue over the gag, please. Blindfolds work, too. The more senses you cut off – sight, speech, hearing – the more you're forced to concentrate on what you're feeling.

Trouble bringing this up? Turn to IDEA 16, *Think kink*, for guidance.

Try another idea...

'The golden rule of kink: only play with people who play nice. Cause the ex who caught you cheating and now has you cuffed and blindfolded ain't comin' back.'
EM and LO, sex agony aunts writing in *The Big Bang*

Defining idea...

135

4. **Nipple clamps.** Experiment first with nipping close to orgasm to see if it's you or your partner's thang. Those who like this really like it.

I'm assuming that when we're not dressing up as naughty schoolgirls and irate headmasters we're all sensible adults and don't need it spelt out that this is potentially dangerous stuff. No tying up for more than half an hour unless you're an expert boy scout. Never leave a tied up person alone without checking on them. No whips near the eyes. Enough already, I hear you say, but I know people who have done scary B&D/S&M stuff with someone that outside of the torture chamber, they wouldn't trust to make them a sandwich. If that's you, get a grip.

**Q** **My husband wants me to pee on him. Hideous. I just can't do it. Why should I?**

*How was it for you?*

**A** *Then don't. But first, and this applies to everything requested in a loving relationship, ask yourself what's going on here. Why does he want it? Why does it disgust you? By exploring, you'll find out a lot about the dynamic of the relationship. Would he settle for a simalcrum? Dr Pam Spurr recommends a bit of role-play before pouring body-temperature tea over your husband while he's blindfolded. Do your best, but ultimately it isn't worth it if it's going to permanently affect how you relate to your husband.*

**Q** **We'd like to experiment with pain, but neither of us felt comfortable with spanking. What do you suggest?**

**A** *There's a really bad sex scene where candles are to the fore starring Madonna and Willem Dafoe in a movie that's best forgotten – it's probably responsible for putting more people off than turning them on. But dripping a drop of hot wax on bare skin, then another, inflicts the right kind of pain, and it feels more grown-up than spanking. Use plain white candles (not perfumed or coloured) that have just been lit (both measures ensure the wax doesn't get too hot). Hold them several feet above the skin, don't drip on the same spot repeatedly, and every now and then test yourself on your own skin to make sure the wax isn't getting too hot.*

# Heading even further south

**Few things in life will earn you so much gratitude for a moderate amount of effort as giving great head.**

It's not rocket science, I hear you say, how can I get it wrong? Boys, you'd be surprised...

I once interviewed a woman who said she'd never enjoyed oral sex because of the biting. Biting? I queried. 'Yes. He sucks so hard that his teeth get in the way.' Her partner mimicked the actions of a blow job on her and it didn't occur to either of them that perhaps sucking wasn't a prerequisite. She didn't feel she could tell him he was getting it wrong so she just avoided oral sex. Nobody's suggesting that you are such a klutz, but experimentation with feedback is essential.

- First, get your partner well and truly motoring with lots of subtle kissing, licking and teasing. This isn't just sexy, it's damn well essential. The clitoris is exquisitely sensitive. This cannot be emphasised enough. It can't take direct stimulation unless its owner is aroused. I don't suggest any man even think of approaching the clitoris (unless specifically invited) until she's thrusting her hips towards you in a pose that tells you quite explicitly what she wants.

Here's an idea for you... **Brush your hand gently through the pubic hair before getting down to business. This grooms out loose pubic hairs – less chance of them ending up between your teeth.**

- Even then, approach slowly. Most of the clitoris, the so-called 'clitoral arms' lie under the skin. Think of the clitoris as an inverted V, with the join being the point where you can see the clitoris. Lying along each labia, pointing downwards towards the perineum, are the 'arms'. Think of a wishbone and stimulate all of it through the skin. The clitoris has more nerves than any other part of the body – thousands more than the penis. Direct attention can frighten it off altogether. Build up to it slowly by working on the arms of the clitoris and always check for a reaction. If she's moving her pelvis away from you – you're going at it too hard.

Here's an idea for you... *'Some men know that a light touch of the tongue, running from a woman's toes to her ears, lingering in the softest way possible in various places in between, given often and sincerely enough, would add immeasurably to world peace.'*
MARIANNE WILLIAMSON, spiritual writer and lecturer

- Try specific moves and ask your lover what variations she likes. Faster, slower, harder, softer. Side to side. Circles?

- Ask questions. Will you show me where…? Do you prefer my tongue hard or soft there? If I keep going just like this, do you think you would come? If not, do you want me to carry on anyway (hey, it's the journey not the destination)?

The secret to giving great oral sex is to remember that the recipient has to be able to concentrate. She has to stay connected to what's happening to her sexually, but still be able to give over control entirely to you. Help her. Make sure she's comfortable. Once she's approaching orgasm, don't distract her by changing what you're doing if you're clearly doing something right.

**Turn to IDEA 27, *Heading south*, for more on cunnilingus.**

*Try another idea...*

## EIGHT THINGS TO DO WITH YOUR TONGUE THAT (SOME) CLITORISES LIKE

This isn't an exhaustive list, but it's based on a poll of women asked for their favourite moves.

- Big flat licks using the whole tongue. The wetter the better.

- Flicking up the edges of the labia, eventually centring on the clitoris.

- Licking upwards repeatedly along the furrows from the vagina to the clitoris, gradually pressing harder every time but never quite reaching the clitoris (stimulating the 'arms', you see).

- Licking gently while pressing down just above the mons (the fleshy bit, at present directly above your nose) with the fingers.

- Circle, circle, flick, flick, flick. Circle, circle, flick, flick, flick.

- Very lazy circles around the clitoris, but not touching it. See how slow you can go. Doing this after a bit of a build-up can drive her mad with longing.

- Suck the clitoris very gently and flick your tongue over it. Or move your tongue slowly up-down, up-down.

- Make your tongue pointy and insert it into the hole rhythmically. (Author's note: This woman liked it, but many men overdo this. Remember, the clitoris is the seat of sex pleasure. Don't overdo tongue penetration unless specifically asked – assuming that their tongue should mimic their penis is the biggest technical mistake men make.)

Try all of these. And at the end when she's approaching orgasm, you'll probably be doing some version of lapping at her clitoris up and down, firmly and rhythmically in a steady and purposeful manner. She'll be bucking against you now. She might like you to hold onto her buttocks or hands tight as she approaches orgasm. It helps her concentrate. Don't change what you're doing at all except perhaps to go a little faster.

**Q**  **He's willing, but he prods at me. Prod, prod, prod. It doesn't do anything for me. What can I tell him?**

*A*  *First I'd suggest that you ask him to go slowly. Really slowly. Slow and steady will eventually work for most women. (Men, if only they knew, don't usually have to go fast until the very end, and even then not always.) The point is that it's hard for him to prod slowly. It's a kind of contradiction on terms and he might automatically then start using the flat-tongue action that's more likely to work for you.*

**Q**  **She just tells me everything's 'fine'. How can I get some feedback?**

*A*  *Blindfold your lover while you're experimenting with different techniques and strokes. Often being blindfolded makes us less self-conscious in reporting how it feels. Try asking her to give each technique a mark out of ten until she gets more confident about saying what she wants or likes.*

*How was it for you?*

## 33

# More on blow jobs

**Can you ever know too much?**

Your blow-job technique comes down to just two things: what you do with your tongue; and what you do with the rest of your body.

What you can do with your tongue is limited, and most of us master the different variations – long slow licks, flicking action, focused pressure on hot spots, etc. – pretty early on.

The magic lies in what you can do with the rest of your body while you're licking and generally pleasuring him with your mouth. Incorporate the principles of kaizen (small changes causing big differences) into your blow-job technique. It's during oral sex more than just about anything else that we tend to stick to the same pattern over and over again. For a good reason – it works for our partner so why chuck away a winning formula? But try mixing it up just a little and you can take a pleasurable experience into the realms of a mind-blowing experience.

Here's an idea for you... **Try stimulating the prostate gland. Men can experiment with this during masturbation and women can use it to give their man a deeper, stronger orgasm.**

## HANDS

■ Touch his chest; squeeze his nipples.

■ Put the fingers of one hand in his mouth so he can suck and lick them.

■ Trace around his anus, balls and perineum (the space between the first two) with your fingers.

■ Slip a well-lubricated finger into his bum and stimulate the prostate gland, which you can feel through the skin of the anterior wall (front), with gentle pressure (give him plenty of warning first that this is your intention). If he doesn't like this, press rhythmically on the perineum, which stimulates the prostate more gently.

■ Hold tight onto his buttocks and spread the cheeks – many men, like women, appreciate the sense of 'stretch'.

Defining idea... **'When authorities warn of the sinfulness of sex, there is an important lesson to be learned: do not have sex with the authorities.'**
MATT GROENING, creator of *The Simpsons*

■ Push up the fleshy area just above the pubic bone or press on it rhythmically. This increases the sensations you're causing with your mouth.

■ Put one hand on the base and another half way up the penis. Stroke the penis with both hands while you take the head of the penis in your mouth.

- Use a vibrator or a bullet on low speed on his perineum while you fellate him.

## EYES

It's oh so simple, but if you don't usually look into your lover's eyes when you go down on him, give it a go. A locked gaze while your mouth slides up and down is powerfully erotic. This is easier in some positions than others so alternate with holding his penis with your hand while you hold his gaze and flick your tongue over the head of his penis.

## LEGS

Straddle his chest as an alternative to the more usual blow-job positions and go on all fours if necessary. This leaves you exposed, but visually it's pretty damn exciting especially if you touch yourself while going south. It also allows him to touch you without any effort whatsoever, which is nice for him. On no account, however, allow him to balance his beer on your butt. That's taking the Michael.

## RHYTHM

Ultimately you find a technique he likes, a groove that he likes and you stick to it. At the most, alternate between two techniques. The only exception to this is when you want to prolong things, which can ensure a stronger, better orgasm for him. Not always, however. Some men's penises appear to get bored with a constant stop–start stop–start method and their orgasm isn't half as explosive as sex manuals would lead you to believe, so unless you know your man, don't overdo the teasing.

As someone once said, 'It's not called a job for nothing.' Turn to IDEA 26, *Handy work*, on hand-job techniques to ring the changes so you can take a break but keep stimulation seamless. Make sure you have plenty of lubricant close by.

*Try another idea...*

147

**Q**  **I tried leaning my head over the edge of the bed while giving him a blow job because I read this was the best way of deep throating. Why didn't it work for me?**

*A*  *Deep throating doesn't exist some will tell you. It certainly doesn't exist in the seventies film starring Linda Lovelace: no woman has a clitoris on the back of the throat. But in the sense that it means taking the whole length of a man's penis into your mouth then it's possible and there isn't, in fact, any big mystique to it. It's a matter of controlling your gag reflex and this might take some practice. The position you tried is based on porn - it's not a great way to start because although it gives a straight line, it's no good if you haven't got the hang of overcoming the gag reflex and, let's face it, lying on your back while being slowly asphyxiated, with no control over the thrusting, is likely to make you feel panicky.*

**Q**  **So how do you deep throat?**

*A*  *You should be in control of the penis, with your hand on the base so that you can be quite sure of this. Keep working up and down, taking the penis into your mouth a bit at a time. When the penis hits the back of your throat, the secret is to get the hang of the breathing. Breathe in as the penis leaves the back of your throat, out when it hits the back of your throat. Go a little further every time. Once you are expert at taking his entire length into your mouth, you can retry with the head-hanging-off-the-bed position, but your lover, who will be controlling the movement, is still going to have to go gently. And never, ever believe what you see in porn or base your performance on it.*

# The love bath

**If you're wise, the bathroom is the place to go to get dirty. Nowhere else in your house will make you feel so spa-cial. (Sorry.)**

Your bathroom should be where the seduction process begins. It's the place to clean up so that you can get down — essential if you don't want to be worrying about little things like being physically repulsive to your mate.

But here's how to really make the most of your bathroom:

### STEP 1: CUT LOOSE

If you find it hard to switch off and are one of those people who always has something else to do, step away from that TV or glass of wine as your evening de-stressor and instead design your own 'transition ritual' where you put aside the stresses of the day and start revving up for a night of passion. It's a lot more likely to get you in the mood for sex than two hours of repeats.

Here's an idea for you... **A good bathroom pastime for women is to position your clitoris under the tap with your legs up the wall. This can result in a powerful orgasm, but it only works if you have a mixer tap and a steady stream of hot water of course.**

Transition rituals are especially important if you work from home (including looking after small children). Make twenty minutes in the bathroom each night the way you send a message to your body that the working day is over and it's time to relax, wind down and play. Your bathroom should be as aesthetically pleasing as possible. Banish plastic toys, keep the lighting soft and wire the bathroom up for sound. Indulge in oils and lotions that make you feel good and let the cares of the day slip away as you bathe. The earlier in the evening you do this, the better. Have 'transitional clothing', too: comfy, light and sensual clothes that you feel comfortable lounging about in. Make this time for yourself – it's a lot more use than a quick shower last thing at night or first thing in the morning.

## STEP 2: HAVE SEX

If you're always too tired for sex, don't wait until it's time to sleep. You know it makes sense. Spending a little time feeling sensual by yourself when you can still keep your eyes open is going to juice you up and leave you feeling frisky. Get your partner to switch off the TV and do something equally life affirming and you'll both be in the mood. Still not convinced? OK, time for...

## STEP 3: MAKE LOVE TO YOUR SHOWER

Oh alright, if you're going to be pedantic, let your shower make love to you. Seriously. If you haven't yet come with the help of your showerhead, what the hell are you doing in there? For women, especially those who have trouble orgasming, directing the flow of water from the showerhead, around and on their clitoris while they're sitting on the side of the bath or lying down results in an easy orgasm. Perhaps because performance pressure is non-existent – you don't have to worry about hurting the showerhead's feelings or taking too long – it works like a charm. When I wrote a piece about the joys of showering back in the early nineties, I was inundated with thank-you letters from women (and a few from their men) who had read the piece and headed straight for the local DIY shop, with fabulous results. So, if you're looking for a good reason to install a decent shower – make it your love life.

Men can enjoy teasing with a showerhead, too – slowly increase the pressure to a point that feels fantastic.

NB Women should only point the showerhead downwards. Water forced up into the vagina carries a very, very small risk of forcing an air bubble where you really don't want one. Not good.

**The bathroom can be a good place to put IDEA 46, *Wait…we said wait*, into practice. You can move the action to the bedroom to really prolong things.**

*Try another idea…*

'Why are women wearing perfumes that smell like flowers? Men don't like flowers. I've been wearing a great new scent guaranteed to attract men. It's called New Car Interior.'
RITA RUDNER, American comedian

*Defining idea…*

How was
it for
you?

**Q** **I tried this lying in the bath underwater and came – eventually.
But it takes a long time. How can I speed things up?**

*A* *It may well take you longer than other methods. That's part of the charm.
If you're in a hurry, try one of the vibrators that are water resistant – the
Jolie is one.*

**Q** **We like the transitional ritual idea. Any more ideas?**

*A* *It works even better as a de-stressor if you do it together. You could
pamper each other in the bathroom. Try rubbing each other down with
gritty exfoliators or smoothing oils over each other's bodies. Aim for
multiple sensory experiences and generally give each other a bit of TLC
before hopping into the shower and having sex. As I keep saying, this is
terrific for couples who are always too tired at 11 p.m. On special
occasions, put some old towels on the bathroom floor and get really mucky.
Dribble honey, chocolate sauce, cream or Bailey's all over each other and
lick it off. And when that gets boring, there's your old friend the
showerhead itching to join the party.*

# 35

# Fight club

**Sexual energy isn't the only flow of energy between a long-standing couple. There's blind fury, too.**

Some couples need a fight to lift their energy enough to have sex, some find their best sex is after a fight and some like 'make-up' sex so much that they pick fights to get turned on.

This last one isn't recommended as it can be emotionally wearing, but you can still use a fight to your best advantage.

## WHEN A FIGHT IS NOT A FIGHT

A fight is not just a fight when it's a way of raising your energy and sparking excitement between the pair of you.

- When you're tired, do you find just having your partner in the room deeply irritating?

Here's an idea for you... **Welcome fights as an opportunity to improve your relationship. A couple's ability to use disagreements to air problems and reach a compromise that brings them closer is one of the signs of a good relationship.**

■ After a period of being happy with your partner, do you feel a sort of pressure building up – a need to get some extreme reaction from them?

■ When you're bored, do you find yourself enjoying an argument about politics, the neighbours, the social significance of Ikea, whatever, as long as you can take up a diametrically opposite position from your mate?

Answer, yes, to any of these? If so, you may be a lover, but you're also a fighter.

■ Do you sometimes feel 'got at', that no matter what you do, your partner is going to seek you out and find fault?

■ Do you have fights that blow up out of nowhere? You're looking out the window, watching the flowers grow, and suddenly you're spitting at each other.

■ Have you noticed that your partner is always particularly loving after a blow-up between you?

Yes? You've got yourself a fighter.

There's no advice here on avoiding fights. A good fight, fought cleanly, can do a lot for a relationship, not least giving you the chance to make up afterwards. There's nothing wrong with harnessing that negative energy and converting it into passion of another type.

**If your fights are fast veering from the recreational to the psychotic, read IDEA 49, *Dealing with burnout.***

*Try another idea...*

But the important thing is to recognise when you're having a fight purely to raise the energy because then you can maximise the fun. When a fight is brewing, decide whether it's about something important? Is one of you making a point fundamental to your relationship? Or is it simply a blow-up, a release of energy, a way of letting off steam at one of the few people that it's 'safe' to lose it with.

If the fight's about something important, you need to know how to fight cleanly and work towards a resolution:

- Don't generalise ('Women always do…'/'You always say…'), test ('If you loved me…'), name-call ('You're horrible') or blame ('You made me…').

- Do stick to the present ('This time…'), stick to the first person ('I feel…' rather than 'You make me…') and look to compromise ('What do we need to both be happy?').

**'Don't go to bed angry. Stay up and fight.'**
PHYLLIS DILLER, comedian

*Defining idea...*

If it's the letting off steam option – wahey! You still have to fight cleanly, but you can also have some fun.

■ Keep to all the rules above.

■ When it's getting heated and you both feel the need for some time out, move the action to the bedroom.

■ The *Kamasutra* suggests eight different ways of biting and four ritual blows before intercourse. It's very big on scratching, too. Proof, if any were needed, that getting physical isn't anything new. Gentle thumping, pushing each other about, getting rough, using your body to express your anger at your mate are all OK. Go for it, but remember it's a bit of fun no matter how angry you are. When we're sexually excited, we have a heightened ability to handle pain – ask the spankees among us. So, be careful not to overdo it just because your partner's not screaming in pain. They simply might not be feeling it yet.

**Q**  **We don't fight. We just niggle at each other. How can we fight 'properly'?**

*How was it for you?*

**A**  *When you find yourself bickering a lot and generally getting on each other's nerves, forget the verbal and get physical. Retire to the bedroom and resolve problems the old-fashioned way – with pillows. Other alternatives if you have a bit more time include:*

- *Naked wrestling. Use lots of baby oil and fight on the bed. The first one to force the other off the bed wins. Make it the best of three falls.*
- *Strip wrestling. First one to get the other naked wins. If you're very unequally matched physically, the larger should be handicapped with a blindfold or one-handed.*
- *Tease torture. One of you is tied to a seat and has to keep a straight face while the other does all he or she can to make you smile.*

**Q**  **Our fights are always serious and bad-tempered. No amount of pillow fights are going to sort us out. What's wrong?**

**A**  *If you're fighting continually, there's almost certainly an underlying resentment – either one of you is angry, or both of you. Couples often put up smoke screens to distract them from facing what's really upsetting them. They'll argue about whether they can afford a new car when what they're really angry about is a lack of sex, commitment or affection. It's a control thing – one person is holding tight to the power in the relationship. The solution? You can try being brave and saying, 'We're arguing about stupid things because we can't agree about this big thing. Let's sort it out.' It's the grown-up thing to do, but if your partner won't talk, all you can do is carry on with your life and as far as possible not react to their attempt to withdraw or control.*

157

# 36

# The joy of shopping

**Who knew that going to the shops could be so good for your love life?**

One in three women in the UK owns a vibrator. For some women, their vibrator is a good and trusty friend with whom they hang out often. For others, it's a tacky bit of plastic skulking at the back of the wardrobe.

This chapter is for the latter, because clearly, although your love life may be buzzing, it's not buzzing literally, and that could mean you're missing a trick. A vibrator is a good and useful thing – a fun thing for both of you. The point of a vibrator is that, yes, it vibrates. Most usefully against your clitoris. To do that it doesn't matter what shape it is, but it helps if it fits on your finger and is pretty discreet so it doesn't get in the way, i.e. not a massive throbbing eight-inch copy of a dick. Funnily enough, what works well for you, will probably work well for your bloke, too. You can use it during sex to run up and down his penis or vibrate against his perineum.

*Here's an idea for you...* **For detailed advice on sex toys of all descriptions, access www.sh-womenstore.com. www.gash.co.uk and www.annsummers.com also have a good selection.**

Here are some vibrators worth checking out. All of these were recommended by the wonderful Kathryn, who works at Sh! (pronounced shush), the first UK sex shop aimed at women.

1. **Your finger – but improved!** The TantraBeam slips over your finger like a ring. It makes your finger vibrate so you can touch skin on skin. Good for people who like to keep things natural.

2. **Remote control.** Toys like the Mantric consist of a small bullet that can be held against any part of your body and a control pack that offers a whole handful of different combinations of stimulation. Or you can buy strap-on vibes that fit discreetly over her clitoris. Try spooning each other while he controls the vibration that she's feeling and ultimately when she comes. If he enters her for the last bit, he'll feel the vibrations, too.

   Another gadget (The Octupus for him and the The Oyster for her) is worn in your pants but is controlled by a remote control that your partner holds. You can give them a blast while they're wandering around the house, talking to the neighbour, having dinner in a restaurant. Not while driving the car.

3. **Rings of confidence.** Cock rings fitted round the penis keep it engorged – good for her, good for him. When the cock ring has a clitoral stimulator attached to it, things get even better. There are lots of these, but one that's definitely worth checking out is the Touchmatic, which only vibrates when it touches the clitoris.

On-off, on-off as he goes in-out, in-out.
Interesting sensation if a bit distracting, but
some people absolutely love it.

Turn to IDEA 37, *Play away*, for
more on sex toys.

*Try
another
idea...*

4. **G-vibes.** There are a whole range of vibrators that are designed to hit your
   G-spot, such as the G-Swirl. This is made from silicone, which suits more people
   than rubber or plastic, even if it's a bit more expensive. Or there's Natural
   Contours Ultime.

Back in the 19th century, vibrators existed before irons and vacuum cleaners.
Electric versions were invented PDQ in order to relieve exhausted doctors who were
often requested to bring off their female patients by hand as a medical procedure to
relieve the symptoms of hysteria. I'm not making this up. Vibrators soon got
popular with the public, since paying your doctor for a hand job was pretty
expensive not to say pretty embarrassing. And things have just got better ever since.

The sex-toy industry improves all the time.
The day I visited Sh! they were excited by the
imminent arrival of a new sort of vibrating
condom, which their tester and her man were
well enthusiastic about. So, if your last venture
into sex shopping was in your teens for a dare
when you emerged with a totally useless red-
and-black garter, do yourself a favour as times
have moved on.

*'Couples have to liberate
masturbation, accept self-
pleasuring in each other,
show one another how to do
it. And if a man can't handle
seeing his lover use a
vibrator, my advice to the
woman is: keep the vibrator
and recycle the man.'*
BETTY DODSON, sex guru

*Defining
idea...*

161

How was it for you?

**Q** **Is it true that you can become desensitised through using vibrators?**

**A** *According to Kathryn, you can. You find you can only come through a certain amount of vibration, delivered by a certain kind of vibrator delivered in an exact way. Which is clearly a pain. The answer is – just like any other sexual partner – don't get lazy with your vibe. Try different kinds of vibrator, alter the way you masturbate, do it through a layer of clothing, take longer and use a lower setting, ask your partner to use it on you. Toys that supply different speeds and settings are good for keeping your genitals on their toes so to speak. If you can only come with your vibrator, experiment with other ways of doing it just for the hell of it. Don't get into a rut.*

**Q** **My last vibrator was really noisy. Have you got any recommendations?**

**A** *Silicone vibrators are better than plastic ones. These days some are whisper quiet. Both Sh! and Gash give a 'loudness' value. But remember the point is to get off – some women need a lot of stimulation and sometimes that means a lot of revs. No namby-pamby vibrator is going to do it for the majority of us. So to hell with the noise, turn up the music!*

# 37

# Play away

**It's safe to say that about ten seconds after some bright cave dweller discovered that the carrot was good to eat, another one worked out that it was good for something else too.**

*Sex toys are some of the oldest toys we've got. And they're not called toys for nothing. They're fun. Great fun. Embrace them.*

Every couple should have their own 'treasure chest' – a special, locked box into which they can dip for a little inspiration. What to put in it? Go shopping. It makes a great date. You might want to go virtual shopping, which is more discreet, and if you get on the net now you can be playing with your new toy within forty-eight hours. Here are some ideas:

## LUBE

And loads of it. Kathryn from my favourite sex shop Sh! says, 'Lesbians have never had the hang up about lube that straight couples do. Using lube doesn't mean you're not a hot vixen. It makes everything better, especially if you want a good long session.'

Here's an idea for you... **If you enjoy him sucking on your clitoris, you may enjoy a clit pump that can be (gently) used to plump up the tissues around the clitoris rendering them exquisitely sensitive.**

Lush is a slightly cheaper version of the famous Liquid Silk, and Probe is a great lubricant for those with allergies. Kathryn recommends Escalate, which contains L-arginine, a natural substance that encourages blood flow and increases sexual pleasure. L-arginine is terrific, but it isn't recommended for people with herpes as there's a small chance it may aggravate them.

If you use any latex products for contraception, don't use Vaseline, baby oil or anything else that will eat up the rubber.

## DILDOS AND STRAP-ONS

'We sell about 30–40% of our strap-ons (harnesses) to heterosexual couples,' says Kathryn, dispelling forever the idea that it's just lesbians with a bad case of penis envy that like waving dildos around the bedroom. She continues, 'It's not a fantasy role-play thing, I don't think. I reckon it's straightforward sensation. Men are getting in touch with their prostate. They like being fucked.' Ladies, look out for slip-on harnesses, like a neat Velcro G-string that gives a snugger fit than many other harnesses, so no flapping about.

There are so many different types of dildos, but the serious choice is silicone – expensive but feels great and heats to body temperature quickly.

And if you want the sensations but can't be bothered with the whole harness thing, look out for the Sh! version of a famous sex toy that they thought they could improve upon. Basically, it's a weighted double dildo where

**Turn to IDEA 36, *The joy of shopping*, for internet addresses for discreet shopping.**

*Try another idea...*

the woman holds one end inside her using her PC muscles, which will give her G-spot stimulation, while the other end penetrates her partner.

## COMING FROM BEHIND

Butt plugs don't provide any motion but they give your anal muscles something to react against when you come. Comforting to wear around the house while doing chores, I'm told. If you like repeated contraction and relaxation of these same muscles then try some beads which when whipped out slowly, or all at once at the point of orgasm, give the prostate a great workout. And, of course, you can buy long thin vibrators specially designed for anal stimulation.

*'There are a number of sexual devices which increase sexual arousal, particularly in women. Chief among these is the Mercedes-Benz 380SL convertible.'*
P. J. O'ROURKE

*Defining idea...*

How was it for you?

**Q**  **Any porn that might hot up our love life?**

*A*  *I wish.*

**Q**  **No, seriously. Isn't there *anything* you can recommend?**

*A*  *Sorry to be so flippant, but I believe that women are just as visual as men when it comes to sex, they just lack anything good to look at. Porn designed to turn on men also turns on women, so experiment. But many of us start to feel crap after a bit – our bodies react physically to it, but the relentless misogyny just gets us down and our minds start to switch off. You could try looking at porn aimed at lesbians, as you might find something that turns you both on. Some adult education videos are supposed to be pretty good. Or maybe you could buy the book* Erotic Home Video *by Anna Span and make your own adult films.*

# 38

# Danger

**Danger is the fastest-acting aphrodisiac.**

*This works better than porn —*
*no kidding.*

In a famous experiment, an attractive scientist interviewed two groups of men. The first group had a standard interview. The second were interviewed after they'd crossed a particularly hairy rope bridge. By the time they were interviewed, their palms were sweaty and their hearts beating fast. This group of men found the same interviewer significantly more alluring. The danger had heightened their sexual response.

In another experiment, male volunteers were each assigned an attractive female assistant. They were told the experiment was investigating electric shock treatments. Some men were told they were in the control group so they wouldn't be receiving shocks. The rest were told they were going to receive painful jolts of electricity. Then they were asked how attracted they felt to their research partner. The ones who were nervously awaiting the shocks found the same women significantly more attractive than the control group.

Here's an idea for you...

**That old chestnut of making a list of six escapades to try and then letting a dice decide which you'll undergo together brings a delicious thrill of Russian roulette to the proceedings.**

I couldn't find any similar experiments carried out on women, but I'm quite sure the results would be pretty well the same. Danger works, most probably, on two levels. First, being scared makes life seem more intense and heightens sexual desire along with everything else. Secondly, it's the old caveman thing.

Share danger together and the bloke gets the chance to look after the female, and she gets to feel all fragile and protected even if she's a cut-throat investment banker who fries balls before breakfast in real life.

No one's suggesting that you set yourself up for anything life threatening, but sharing adventures together will do the job – especially physical adventures. Adventures count as anything that gets your adrenaline flowing. It needn't necessarily be dangerous. You're simply seeking a shared experience that gets both of your hearts thumping.

**SOME IDEAS**

**Soft core**
- Go to Alton Towers, Disneyland or anywhere with fast, high rides.
- Dare each other.
- Have sex where you might just be seen.
- Stay the night somewhere reputedly haunted, but definitely creepy.
- Shop at a sex shop together.

**Hard core**

- Have sex when other people could definitely see you. (Be subtle – you don't want to frighten the horses or get arrested.)
- Go white-water rafting, bungee jumping or parachute jumping.
- Take your clothes off at midnight at the end of your street.
- Go to amateur night at your local comedy club together. Stand up and be funny.

**Use your imagination. Combine danger with secrecy in IDEA 42, _Dirty little secrets_, for some extremely bonding experiences.**

_Try another idea..._

Finally, actively trying to instil a sense of danger to your lives should act as an aphrodisiac, but to strengthen the bond between you and not just the sexual energy. Look at the totality of the life you're building together. If you're experiencing sexual doldrums, is that because your life has become stale and everything's routine? As a couple, are you building the sort of life you want? Is it time to stop playing at being dangerous and start taking some genuine risks with the intention of improving your life? Is it time to move to the country, move to the city, move jobs, have a child, adopt a child, travel round the world, give up work and live off the land, start a new business, live on a beach? Sure, it's frightening. Sure, it might backfire. But if you can agree on a huge life-changing, scary-as-hell decision together and you succeed, your satisfaction with each other should be sky high. And there's nothing like feeling that you've worked hard and succeeded at something with your soulmate for giving your libido a bit of a boost.

_'My ultimate fantasy is to entice a man to my bedroom, put a gun to his head and say "make babies or die".'_
RUBY WAX, writer and comedian

_Defining idea..._

How was
it for
you?

**Q**   **My partner is just not the type for this. He's an intellectual kind of bloke and all your ideas are out-doorsy. What else can I try?**

**A**   *Hmm. I see your point. Try doing things differently, possibly pushing him out of his comfort zone a little. For example, suggest that you meet at the Prada in Madrid on a particular Saturday next month. You have to get there alone. You're not allowed to confer in any way. Travel separately and check-in to separate hotels. Meet. It's not exactly dangerous but you'll have each had separate experiences, met different people and had to think outside the box – a first step to living more exciting lives.*

**Q**   **We have different danger levels. Going horse riding is pretty scary for me, but my boyfriend wants to go parachute jumping. Surely being terrified won't help?**

**A**   *That's sort of the idea, but for goodness sake don't be foolhardy or you'll end up hating him. Start with horse riding. Go at your own speed. Competence builds confidence. Make sure he realises that horse riding is just as scary for you as parachute jumping is for him.*

# 39

# 'Let a woman be a woman and a man be a man'

**There's a bloke in the States called David Deida who has some interesting ideas as to why sex goes off the boil.**

There's nothing particularly new about his ideas, but the way he packages his theories is pretty compulsive.

We're equal, but we're knackered. Even long-standing relationships are crumbling under the strain of couples overworking. Latest figures show that the divorce rate is inching towards half of all marriages.

But according to Deida, life doesn't have to be this way. Deida says women aren't drudges, but passionate, vital, thrilling creatures who given the chance should be living a life of rich emotional complexity. In order to shine, they need the love of what Deida calls 'the superior man'. A strong, focused, individual striving towards his destiny. According to Deida, when men are strong and women can rely on them, passionate intensity isn't far away. What's wrecking our sex lives, he says, is too much equality. Yes, you read that right.

**David Deida has written several books, including *The Way of the Superior Man* (for men) and *It's a Guy Thing* (for women). You can check out www.deida.com to see if his ideas are likely to appeal.**

'The bottom line of today's fifty–fifty relationship,' Deida continues, 'is that men and women are clinging to a politically correct sameness even in bed and that's when sexual attraction disappears. The love may be strong, but the sexual polarity fades.' According to Deida, men and women have both a masculine and feminine side or 'polarity'. It's fine for men to get in touch with their feminine side (real men do cry), and women with their masculine (they're brilliant in the boardroom). She can be the breadwinner, he can look after the kids, but if they want fireworks to continue, he has to be someone she can rely on and trust, and she has to remove the shoulder pads as soon as she walks through the front door.

**WHAT'S A SUPERIOR MAN?**

Deida's roots appear to be in the men's movement, the reaction to feminism, which tries to help men make sense of our crazy, mixed-up world, and their role in it. He believes that a man isn't really happy unless he's striving towards his goal, whatever that is. When he loses sight of his goal, he needs 'time out' – what in other cultures would have been called a 'vision quest' – sort of metaphorically speaking going into the desert and beating his drum until he finds his way again. Unless he finds his way he's no use to anyone, least of all his bird. This is why she has to understand the importance of his quest. She can also help him be a superior man by 'challenging him', i.e. not putting up with any shit. No lying about watching Sky Sports when he should be looking for a job, say. No nights down the pub to distract him from the fact that he hasn't written a word of that best-selling novel. Deida calls it 'challenging'. It sounds like plain old 'nagging' to me. Anyway, there's lots in his work about how a man can become superior, but here's a couple of ways he can be superior in direct relation to the woman in his life.

Turn to IDEA 52, *Are you sexually mature*, to check just how evolved you are when it comes to relating to each other.

Try another idea...

You'll know you're a superior man when you stop trying to control a woman's emotions and you listen to her. You do your best to understand her feelings and don't walk away from them. You don't offer useless advice when she wants you as a sounding board, but give her a hug. You make her laugh a lot. You're your own man. You listen, you take advice on board and then you do what you think best. You're trustworthy. You do what you say you'll do. And when you don't, you own up and take responsibility for it. You pay attention to your partner. You know that thirty minutes fully concentrating on her is worth four hours half-listening and fiddling with the remote. Got that?

Deida's ideas aren't for everyone, but I've met and interviewed couples for whom his ideas work well. The couples are equal, but they accept the sexes are different and that a man and a woman can't be everything to each other. Deida's ideas give a way of negotiating the contradictions of being a 'good bloke' and being a 'new man', which lots of men struggle with. If you can handle the New Age language, of course.

'Both men and women are bisexual in the psychological sense. I shall conclude that you have decided in your own minds to make "active" coincide with "masculine" and "passive" with "feminine". But I advise against it.'
SIGMUND FREUD

Defining idea...

How was it for you?

**Q Let me get this right. I have to wander around like a drippy hippy, supporting his 'quest'?**

*A No, he can support your quest. Couples can switch polarity completely, and as long as that works for you, and the polarity is present, fine. But most of us switch between polarities and the danger lies where a woman is expected to carry too much of the masculine energy and can't switch back into being feminine. Who can doubt that many women these days are dazed and confused, attempting to do too much and taking out their frustration on their men? Your aspirations are important, too. But for your relationship's sake, you need to keep polarity and keep in touch with your 'sense of identity'.*

**Q And that would be exactly?**

*A A woman should nourish her femininity at every opportunity – dancing, music, yoga, hanging out with girlfriends, orgasmic sex. All of these will support your feminine essence, and making time for them should be a priority if you want your relationship to stay strong. Do some nourishing every day. Have a long luxurious bath, dress in silk or other sensuous fabric, massage with scented oils, play your favourite music and dance like no one's watching, or stare at the stars. Spend as much time as possible with supportive women friends, as they can often see what you need better than you can. And before you ask, your partner has to actively help you find the time for these things. That's the superior way.*

# 40

# Tantric sex

**Not just a load of old joss sticks.**

If you've absolutely had it with your partner's idea of foreplay being a quick tap on your shoulder and a hopeful expression, then it's time to go Tantric.

To the student of Tantra, sex is sacred, a means of accessing your spirituality and a way to meditate, transcend your problems and reach a happier more blissful state. For those of us who don't have the time or inclination to study Tantric sex in any great depth, it can still add a lot. It teaches sex is important, and by clearing time to undergo a few of the simpler rituals you declare to each other 'Hey, our sex life is a priority.'

Tantric sex teaches you to concentrate on your lover and on the sensations that you're feeling. Forget the orgasm. The journey not the arrival is what's important. And for that reason alone, Tantra can be liberating and mind-altering, even if you don't get into it the whole way.

Here's an idea for you...

**Try dreaming of rainforests, droning music, an overflowing bank account...once you're out of Sting-world though, Google 'Tantric', but set your porn filter to 'Kill'.**

## RITUAL ONE: CREATE A 'TEMPLE OF LOVE'

A really simple method of foreplay is to make your bedroom a sensual haven quite different from the rest of your home. You don't have to opt for lurid leopard prints and black walls – unless you like that, of course – but take a long look at your bedroom as if seeing it for the first time. Does is say 'love', 'passion', 'excitement'? Is it a room devoted to the two of you?

First, think about what's in the room. Would you say that the television contributed to improving your love life? Unless you mainly use it to watch porn, probably not. Perhaps you spend more time watching it than talking to each other. If you want to keep the TV, find a scarf to cover it as a mental signal that you're switching off from the outside world. Similarly, ban work paraphernalia – piles of clothes waiting to be ironed, family photographs, anything that takes your attention away from each other and onto your responsibilities. Repair and clean tatty or old furnishings. Clear away clutter. Throw open the windows and let some fresh air circulate. This room is a reflection of your relationship – it's where you spend the most time with each other. It should sparkle.

Finally, create a love altar. Find a picture of you both together that symbolises the best of your relationship. When you look at it, you should feel warm and compassionate towards your partner and strong as a couple. Place it in a nice frame where you can see it easily every day. Keep fresh flowers next to the photograph and candles – anything that you have to tend regularly and pay attention to – as a

physical reminder that your relationship needs
similar care and tending. Make sure there are
soft lights in your bedroom and soft music to
hand, comfortable cushions or duvets that you

**Turn to IDEA 41, *In out in out,*
for more Tantric-type ideas.**

*Try
another
idea...*

can sink into, and a bedroom should always be comfortably warm so hanging
around with few clothes on doesn't make you shudder.

None of this is genius level, but think of yours and your friends' bedrooms. How
many have been designed with sensuality, luxury, comfort and *sex* in mind? Your
bedroom should be a place that's welcoming to both of you, so that you look
forward to hanging out in the only place where most couples can be truly intimate
and private with each other.

## RITUAL TWO: THINK YOURSELF IN LOVE

Tantric sex depends on visualisation to build sexual energy. As your lover begins to
caress you, feel how much they love you. Imagine their love for you flowing from
their fingers and hands and nurturing you.
Melt into their embrace. When they kiss you,
feel that with each kiss they are showing how
much they love you. Imagine the sexual energy
that you are creating between you is visible as a
red or pink light emanating from your genitals
and surrounding you like a force field of love.
As your partner touches you, imagine that your
arousal is growing like a great wave of light. See
it as fire or energy emerging from your deep

*'The relation of man to a
woman is the flowing of two
rivers side by side,
sometimes mingling, then
separating again, and
travelling on. The relationship
is a life-long change and life-
long travelling.'*
D. H. LAWRENCE

*Defining
idea...*

177

pelvis and adding to the force field surrounding and supporting you. As you begin to have sex, imagine the energy passing upwards from the base of your spine to your heart and feel this energy as love around your heart – feel it as joy – and imagine it reaching out and surrounding your partner's heart. Then, as you get more excited, imagine the energy being drawn upwards and flowing out through the top of your head.

That's the way to enlightenment, but it takes a bit of practice. Look on the bright side, with all that visualising going on at least you won't be thinking about who's doing the school run tomorrow.

How was it for you?

**Q    It feels good, but it doesn't feel that special. Why not?**

A    *Tantric sex is a discipline – with practice, the feelings grow. If you believe in the basic concept that sex is a way to deepen and enrich your life, then invest in a good book about Tantric sex.*

**Q    Does it mean you can last for hours?**

A    *Er, yes. That's part of it. With practice, couples can keep going for hours if that's what they want. But even Sting, the most famous proponent of Tantric sex, cracked the joke that when he'd gone public about his seven-hour sex sessions, he hadn't mentioned that five and a half hours were taken up with dinner and a movie. Don't get too attached to the outcome of lasting for ages. That's not the point.*

# 41

# In out, in out

**Breathing. You do it every single minute of your life. Boy, have you been taking it for granted.**

With the least amount of effort, you can turn the simple act of breathing into a way to heighten sexual pleasure and get closer to your partner. Pretty damn useful.

There isn't a single sexual tradition or sex guru that doesn't have something to say about breathing. Taking deep breaths supplies more oxygen to the brain and muscles, which both deepens your sexual response and aids relaxation.

## FIRST THINGS FIRST

Next time you're having sex, breathe as normal and observe what you do. Olivia St Claire, author of *302 Advanced Techniques for Driving a Man Wild in Bed*, says most women breathe shallowly when they're having sex. Taking deeper breaths should deepen sensations, but can be hard to remember when approaching orgasm. At that point, try instead to take rapid, deep breaths through your mouth rather than your nose.

Here's an idea for you... **If you're wound up, try using breathing techniques to de-stress yourself. They're the basis of all meditation, as well as improved sex.**

Men, too, can deepen sensation by breathing deeply. Both of you imagine that you are drawing air down through your lungs into your pelvic area. Concentrating your attention there via your breathing can help build excitement.

## THE 'COMPLETE' BREATH

Yogic breathing is to draw breath in, hold the breath in your lungs, exhale and then pause before breathing again. Practice this and then breathe in for one count, hold for four counts, breathe out for two counts and pause. Repeat this until it comes naturally.

## FOCUSING ON LURVE

In the Tantric tradition, the inward breath is associated with energy and the outward breath with consciousness. This is a good basis for a mini-meditation session before you make love. Concentrate on taking in energy in with each inward breath and, with each outward breath, bringing your concentration to bear on how you're feeling right here, right now.

Defining idea... *'There is only one real antidote to the anguish engendered in humanity by its awareness of inevitable death: erotic joy.'* BENEDIKT TASCHEN, German publisher

## BREATHING IN UNISON

I was once asked to write a piece about improving communication between lovers. My partner and I were given around twenty techniques to try out that were supposed to help improve our relationship. One was to lie in bed, 'spooned' around one another, and simply breathe in unison. During the two weeks that we undertook our 'research', we spent hours writing lists, talking deeply, having sex at odd times and in odd positions, massaging each other and even venturing to a salsa class, but probably nothing worked as elegantly as the simple breathing exercise. Nothing else stuck either. Try it once a day (oh, alright then, as often as you remember), in bed or out, clothed or not. Hold onto each other and regulate your breaths. Let thoughts drift away as they float into your mind. Just be with each other.

For those who like this, try heart breathing. Sit on your bed in a comfortable position facing each other. Place your hands flat on your chest between your breasts (above the heart chakra). Close your eyes. Now breathe as detailed under 'The complete breath' above. Imagine you're drawing love in with each breath and, while holding it in your lungs, feel it nourishing your body and spirit. Finally, when you breathe out imagine your breath leaving your body as a wave of love rolling over and around your partner. Open your eyes and look at your partner while you breathe together.

If you want to make sex more spiritual, turn to IDEA 40, *Tantric sex.*

*Try another idea...*

'**Your breath is a bridge between your body, feelings and thoughts, your energy, your past and your present. How we breathe directly affects every cell of our body, and it also influences how we feel emotionally. As such, the breath is also a vehicle for expansion and ecstasy.'**
LEONORA LIGHTWOMAN, Tantric teacher and author

*Defining idea...*

181

How was it for you?

**Q** **Very relaxing, but how does this relate to improving sex?**

**A** *The more relaxed or 'open' that you are, the more likely you are be to be in touch with your body. Breathing deeply and feeling yourself 'expand with love', helps you feel more powerfully aware of your sexuality and anyone else's who happens to be in the room. David Deida says that deep breathing is especially important for women, and is one of the ways of maintaining their feminine polarity. He urges us as often as possible – all day preferably – to 'breathe with the same open pleasure you would if your lover's body were pressing against yours'. Not easy, but work at it and Deida promises both 'men and women will be attracted to your radiance and respectful of your depth'. In other words, you'll be more serene and less stressed, which does indeed tend to be more attractive than the alternative – a fried wreck. But seriously, imagining you are relaxing into a loving embrace during the day, especially when things get frantic, acts to make you think of your lover, sex, hugs and physical closeness – all the good things in life. And yes, it boosts your libido.*

**Q** **I start to get giddy after a while. Is this OK?**

**A** *This proves you're doing it right. These exercises or similar ones are the basis of all the mystic traditions. Because breathing is the one thing we can't forget to do, 'working with the breath', basically becoming conscious of our breathing, has been used since time began as a means of making us aware that we are alive in this moment, and there won't be another one quite like it. Recalling that self-evident fact is a powerful way of appreciating life in general and your lover in particular.*

# Dirty little secrets

**Why every couple needs some.**

Think about the best holiday you've ever had together. Those shared memories can't help but make you smile. And no one else would understand them but you two. This chapter is about the sex equivalent of the perfect holiday.

What you're aiming to do is create a stronger bond between you in the simplest way possible. You know something about your partner that no one else knows. Oh, OK, you two have secrets already – you know hundreds of things about your partner that no one else knows. But, by sharing sexual secrets, you become even closer. That's because you underline the uniqueness of your relationship – *no one else* but you two knows these secrets. And, of course, creating the secrets is bloody good fun.

Here's an idea for you... **Create new sexual secrets. Talk about old ones that you've shared. On no account share the sexual secrets you had with another partner. That's missing the point.**

A good example of creating a sexual secret is to shave off each other's pubic hair. This is still mildly shocking, though God knows why with the ubiquity of the Brazilian wax where both sexes let total strangers loose on them. Whatever. Besides the frisson of naughtiness, there's a practical reason to try shaving. Being hairless increases sensations, especially during oral sex. Plus, in a crowded room, you'll be the only one who knows why they're squirming about so much in their seat when the hair starts to regrow. But despite the itch, it's well worth trying at least once because it really redefines the meaning of 'intimacy'. First trim with small nail scissors (you see why this is so intimate), then bathe and then lather up with hair conditioner. Next, apply liberal amounts of shaving gel, and use disposable razors to carefully shave off the hair. Use your hand to smooth down areas like the labia to get a good line. Women, ask your man for advice – they know more about this than you do. You could experiment with heart shapes or trimming initials if you don't want to go the whole way. Apply hypoallergenic lotion afterwards to soothe it all down, which also helps when the hair's growing back.

Besides the risqué, using daily everyday objects to filthy effect is another good ruse. For instance, use lipstick to draw around your penis, nipples or labia. Have your partner lick and suck it off. That takes a lot of suction and you'll never hear the word 'lipstick' together again without looking at each other knowingly.

You could also try wearing each other's underwear to work. For women, wearing a loose pair of boxers under a skirt let's the air circulate where it normally never gets to go and makes you feel more open in every sense of the word. For men, the feeling of constriction that comes from tight feminine panties under your business suit can be arousing – as well as all the other associations and images that will flash through your mind throughout the day.

**Need help persuading your lover? Turn to IDEA 16, *Think kink.***

*Try another idea...*

Take this one step further and play around with cross-dressing. Wear each other's clothes in bed. You'll hate it or love it, but if you love it, you might be surprised at how much you love it. For men especially, breaking one of the last great heterosexual taboos (dressing as a woman) is a hugely liberating experience. Remember, no one knows but you two.

Need more inspiration? Go to a naturist beach together, make a porn short, photograph each other nude or have sex on the steps of your local library (make it a quickie!) – risky, but it will make you smile every time you drive to the supermarker!

And, of course, don't break the first rule of secrets. You don't tell. Ever.

*'The real fountain of youth is to have a dirty mind.'*
JERRY HALL, actress and model

*Defining idea...*

How was
it for
you?

**Q   Nothing you suggest appeals. Maybe we're not the secretive type. Anything else we can try?**

A    *Of all the ideas in this book, this one has the most potential to be ridiculous. Sex makes us vulnerable, and that can make us feel foolish. If you're bereft of inspiration I suggest you think about someone you sit next to at work or an old friend. Then think of something sexual that if they knew about you'd die of mortification. You don't have to have done it – yet – you just have to be going red at the thought of them seeing you doing it. Got someone in mind? Well, there you go. That's the basis for a secret. Some things about our sex lives we wouldn't want anyone to know about, but we open ourselves up a lot by letting one other person share them. And that's sexy. A bit squirm-making, but sexy, too.*

**Q   I like having sexual secrets from my wife – it turns me on. I'm not really interested in sharing secrets with her though, it feels a bit childish. Am I being selfish?**

A    *It might be that you need to work on your sexual maturity a little. It seems like your wife is willing to share her secrets (which might be a big effort for her), so perhaps you need to try harder to do the same in return.*

# 43

# Just say 'no'

**There's saying 'no' and there's saying 'no' nicely. Two very different things.**

Every relationship has its sexual deserts when sex is off the cards. Here's how to negotiate your way through them so no one gets too hurt.

Sometimes we simply want to say 'no'. We might be tired. We might be feeling sad. We might be preoccupied with something else. If your partner approaches you and you feel ambivalent about having sex, my best advice is to go along with it for a while and try to get yourself in the mood (with their help, of course). If, however, you fail to rise onto that wave of lust, all you can do is gaze into their eyes tenderly and say, 'Sorry, it isn't working for me tonight, but I promise that tomorrow we'll do the deed.' Sex therapists pretty much agree that rejection is easier to take if there's a definite date set for a retry. As a consolation prize and to give them the human contact that we all crave (and which probably instigated their shuffle across the bed in the first place), you could hold your partner while they masturbate to orgasm. (And if you're not comfortable masturbating in front of each other, maybe you ought to think about why not. It's a useful habit.)

Here's an idea for you... **If you and your partner haven't had sex for a month, sit down, look into his/her eyes and ask why. The longer you go without sex, the easier it becomes to do without it. The more you do it, the more you'll want to.**

But what if you know that tomorrow you're not going to want to have sex either? What if this one's going to run and run? A genuine sexual desert where it's been months and months and months, and you don't need so much to negotiate it as buy a map and a compass and start charting the unknown continent. First things first. Do you both want to emerge from your desert and find your oasis?

## 'YES' TO THE OASIS?

Is there a medical reason that one or both of you has gone off sex? Is it because one or both of you is having a mid-life crisis? Deal with that and do the following.

## 'NO' TO THE OASIS

Tricky one this. You've gone off sex. You don't fancy your partner anymore. You can't be bothered to try. When they approach you, you simply don't want to do it.

Don't let sex be an *ad hoc* arrangement. Decide on a time when you're going to get physical and then do all you can to get yourself in the mood, such as a bath, delicious food, candles or a chat. Enjoy each other. Don't expect mind-bending lust – mildly being up for it is good enough. If it's been a long time and you're a bit nervous about having sex, go back to basics. It doesn't matter what you do as long as you're physically close. Being physically close without having penetrative sex can eventually kick start your libido. In fact, when you've been together for a while, you often need physical proximity to *start* feeling desire. In other words, you can' t hang around waiting for an overwhelming wave of lust to wash over you or you'll wait a long time. Start having sex and let Mother Nature take her course.

**If it's your partner who rejects your advances then read IDEA 12, *The love's there but the lust's gone AWOL.*** *Try another idea...*

The bottom line is, if you can't be bothered to do all you can to get yourself and your partner in the mood for sex then you're a rotten lover.

**Can't be bothered with sex? Read IDEA 9, *Get over yourself.*** *...and another*

What's loving about a person who doesn't at least try? This is brutal, but it's true. Perhaps you're right to take your lover's constancy for granted even when you're not putting out, trusting that they'll stick by you. But they're almost certain to get depressed and unconfident – both traits are hell to live with and unlikely to endear them to you. Keeping your sex life extant is as important for your mental health as theirs.

'Marriage, if it is to survive, must be treated as the beginning, not as the happy ending.'
FEDERICO FELLINI

*Defining idea...*

How was it for you?

**Q** **I've been wandering the sexual desert following the birth of our children, but there's no oasis in sight. How much longer before the camel train arrives?**

*A* *There are usually two main problems here. The first is that either or both of you are simply not putting the relationship above other things, notably the kids. Time for some deep talking then. Personally, I think that although parents would quite happily lay down their lives for their children, rarely are such sacrifices called for to keep them healthy and happy. If you're sacrificing your relationship for your kids, then that's your decision, but it's probably the wrong one.*

**Q** **I've told my partner a million times that to get in the mood I need a bit of a chat, lots of foreplay, some build up. So why does he persist in grabbing me when I'm unloading the dishwasher, muttering 'fancy a bit' like a dirty old man and then getting huffy when I tell him to sod off?**

*A* *He probably hates having to go through your proscribed dance of seduction. This isn't all about sex. He's resentful that you get to decide when and how you'll have sex. There's a power struggle between you two that's being enacted over the battleground that is your dishwasher. Your partner may just yearn for a quickie and not know how to ask you for one. Would it be the end of the world if you succumbed? Of course, if sometimes you do succumb, then there's nothing complicated or psychological going on at all. He's just chancing his arm on the principle that if one time out of fifty you say yes, he might get lucky again.*

# It's not all in your mind

**If you've gone off sex, it may be time to see your doctor.**

*Our bodies affect our libido much more than we'd care to admit.*

It's an odd person that goes throughout life with the same level of sexual brio. Our income, lifestyle, confidence levels and any medication we've been prescribed by our doctors all affect how much desire we feel. But the big daddy that affects our libido is a hormonal change. Hormones determine so much about our lives, from how attractive we look (ovulating women get better looking) to the sorts of films we want to watch (new parents of both sexes have trouble with war movies).

This is why it's so odd that when we go off sex we don't head straight to the doctor for a check-up. What's even odder is how little use most of our doctors are if we actually do get there. I'm not getting at GPs, but they have limited resources and these tend to be focused on patients with cancer rather than those who only feel like sex once a month. So you'll have to do a lot of medical research yourself if you feel that your health is standing in the way of your love life. The internet is a wonderful thing, just don't start sending away for things that promise to make your penis bigger.

Here's an idea for you... **A lack of desire is one of the major symptoms of depression. It's also a side effect of some antidepressant drugs. What we call a catch-22. In cases of mild to moderate depression, exercise has been shown to be as effective as medication and might be well worth trying seriously.**

We have very limited space, but this chapter is going to give you a few ideas to start you off on your own road to discovery *vis-à-vis* your body and provide you with some key words to type into the search engine. 'I want to have sex more' isn't a great thing to let Google know about, not unless you want a lot of strange men in Minneapolis trying to get friendly with you.

## ARE YOU TAKING ANY MEDICATION?

If you are, you really do need to speak to your GP. Many different kinds of medication, including those for heart conditions and depression, can lower your libido. Some forms of the contraceptive pill also make you less interested in sex. Your GP may be able to change your prescription, but they won't be able to do that if you don't tell them there's a problem in the first place.

## YOU'VE HAD A KID

The theory is that women go off sex so that they can concentrate on one baby's survival before conceiving another. My theory is that it's their own survival they're concerned about. Don't believe the books that tell you recovery only takes six weeks; but it doesn't take two years either. Having said that, many women do go off sex for literally years after giving birth – a weird physical and psychological inertia takes over. Eventually, you've just got to get back in the saddle and use every trick to rebuild your libido from the ground up.

If you're a man who's gone off sex big time since your child's been born, two things: you could be a terrific big-time bonder producing tons of a hormone that actually suppresses testosterone in new fathers, making you happy to hang around the metaphorical campfire

**Read IDEA 49, *Dealing with burnout*. The mind can have a profound effect on the body. Maybe your state of mind is affecting yours.**

Try another idea...

with your missus and the little 'un rather than, say, nipping to the cave next door for a bit of how's your father. In which case, your libido will come back. Alternatively, you could have deep-rooted psychological hang-ups along the Madonna/whore axis. In which case, you need therapy.

## YOU'RE OF A CERTAIN AGE

By this, I mean anything from about thirty-five on. For women, that's when the perimenopause kicks in – the period (no pun intended) leading up to the menopause proper. Your hormonal balance alters and although some women experience nothing at all, others are forgetful, moody, irritable and, of course, less interested in sex. Your GP may be able to prescribe HRT depending on your hormonal levels, but you may not be happy with this. There are a host of herbal remedies that can help maintain libido in the years up to and following the menopause. Try black cohosh and red clover.

*'I once made love for an hour and fifteen minutes. But it was the night the clocks were set ahead.'*
GARY SHANDLING, American comedian

Defining idea...

How was it for you?

**Q**  **Do men have a male menopause?**

*A*  *It seems that some do – the so-called andropause. So far, it's not been proven, but what has been found is that some men do respond to testosterone medication and regain their lust along with their love for life.*

**Q**  **Would Viagra help me get my libido back?**

*A*  *It might, but Viagra isn't completely without problems. One of the most obvious problems is that in a relationship where a man has had problems with arousal, his sudden priapic and demanding new persona can cause havoc. Read up on all the pros and cons and discuss it with your partner and doctor beforehand.*

**Q**  **I've put on a lot of weight and thought that was the reason I was going off sex.**

*A*  *It could be, but the weight loss might be a symptom of a condition that is robbing you of sexual desire. Low thyroid hormones is one possibility. So is diabetes or the menopause. Go to your doctor for a check-up and make sure you discuss your low libido as well as your weight gain.*

# 45

# Pressure – it's not a dirty word

**Or rather, if you're doing it right, it can be.**

For most, sex is the main course of lovemaking. Oh, OK, for most, sex is more of a quick snack. But for times when (to push the meal metaphor to the limit) you want to feast on a banquet of love, there is massage.

You don't need to be self-conscious about massaging each other. It doesn't have to be of a professional standard because what you lack in technique you can more than make up for by what is called 'loving intention'; your total focus on your partner's relaxation and pleasure will do lots of good.

First, select your oil. You can buy massage oils premixed or create your own blend by adding eight to ten drops of oil (or a mixture of oils) to three dessertspoons of a base oil such as almond. Good oils for sensual massage are geranium, which is uplifting and grounding; lavender, which is relaxing and soothing; sandalwood, which is warming and encouraging; and ylang ylang, which is sensual and erotic. Burning the same combination of oils as you massage will heighten the experience for your lover.

**Maintain skin-to-skin contact throughout the massage. Cup one hand on your lover's back while you pour more oil so that the back of your hand maintains this contact.**

Choose a warm, comfortable place in your home. Put on some gentle music and lower the lights. Take a bath or shower together. The masseur (or masseuse) should dress in light comfortable clothes and make their lover comfortable lying on their front.

Take some oil – and you should have liberal amounts to hand – and warm it between your palms. Then start working the oil into your partner's back. Use firm gliding strokes over the large muscles of the shoulder blades, then work down the sides to the base of the spine and then work upwards using the balls of your thumbs to apply pressure on either side of the spine. The secret of applying pressure is to channel the strength of your body through the balls of your thumbs. Lean into your lover's body but apply pressure only to the meaty parts of the body (but not the belly). Don't apply pressure on hard bony areas.

Continue with sweeping movements alternated by gentle pressure across the back, buttocks and the back of legs. Use long strokes along the arms and gently pull at each finger in turn. Try different pressures. Use fists to apply heavier kneading movements to the buttocks. Apply very light blows across the back. Then alternate with gentle fingertip stroking.

Don't worry about your technique, just concentrate on your lover's body and giving it pleasure. Ask for a little feedback. For example, does your partner want a gentler or firmer stroke? But don't talk too much. Allow your partner to relax into the massage.

Ask your partner to turn over. Holding their head steady with your knees and massaging their face is particularly relaxing. Don't apply heavy pressure to the stomach. Brush but don't directly touch their genitals – the oils may irritate sensitive areas. Anyway, the point is to build sensual pleasure for you both, not necessarily to move onto sex. Judge how your partner feels. Are they giving the impression that this is turning them on? Or is it so relaxing that they want to curl up in your arms and sleep. If you're not sure, ask them, and don't let your wishes come through either way. Making it clear you expect sex in return for giving massage isn't considered sporting.

**Explore your potential for touch in IDEA 13, *Coming over all touchy-feely.***

*Try another idea...*

## SHORT CUT TO BLISS

If you don't have the time to indulge in a full body treat, give a foot massage instead.

Bathe your lover's feet. A few drops of peppermint oil in a basin refresh instantly and keeps things fresh for you. Then ask them to sit while you kneel at their feet, with a towel over your knees to cradle each foot in turn. Massage oil over one foot. Apply pressure through your thumbs systematically all over the soles of the feet. Concentrate particularly on the fleshy parts of each toe in turn and gently pull and rotate each one. If you're feeling particularly loving, wipe the oil from your lover's nails and give them a pedicure (men, too). Men, painting your lover's toe nails means she remembers your heavenly foot massage every time she catches sight of her tootsies – an easy way of garnering brownie points.

*'To lovers, touch is metamorphosis. All the parts of their bodies seem to change, and seem to become something different and better.'*
JOHN CHEEVER, American Writer

*Defining idea...*

How was it for you?

**Q**   **We don't often have time for the whole nine yards. Any shortcuts?**

*A*   *You can use acupressure in seconds during sex to heighten your lover's sexual pleasure. The ancient Chinese teach that pressing acupressure points is like a concentrated massage, releasing tension and building pleasure. One spot directly above the penis or clitoris and one on each side activates points that are linked to increasing sexual energy and by pressing these you arouse your lover faster. There's another series of three points in the front of the thighs in the crease where the pubis meets the thigh. Pressing there heightens sensitivity, especially when you're giving oral sex. Finally, imagine a line drawn between the pubic area and the hipbone on each side. Pressing along 'the crease' there increases pleasurable feelings in the genitals. Press firmly and relax – don't press any of these points for much more than a couple of minutes at a time.*

**Q**   **I find that receiving massage tickles and it's distracting. Any advice?**

*A*   *Your lover needs to exert more pressure. Ask them to lean in harder. Give them feedback until you receive the level of pressure you want.*

**Q**   **Why don't I like giving massage? I don't like receiving it much either…**

*A*   *There could be all sorts of reasons for this, but let's cut to the chase – a possible solution. Perhaps you feel embarrassed. Try using the god/goddess or priest/priestess fantasy. If you're receiving massage, you're the god/goddess and it's the greatest pleasure and honour for your priest/priestess to be serving you. Reverse this if you're the priest or priestess serving the deity. Get out of your head and concentrate on the physical.*

# 46

# Wait. We said wait!

**Delay orgasm – a.k.a. 'peaking' – and you'll know the true meaning of 'climb every mountain'.**

Is there a woman alive who on approaching the big 'O' hasn't muttered, 'Don't stop, for God's sake don't stop'? A woman's biggest fear is that with the winning line in sight, he changes his stroke, everything goes pear-shaped and she doesn't make it.

So, when a woman feels herself on the edge of an orgasm she'll rush her way there. It's hard-earned and she wants it now. But here's another way for her to do it. On the point of orgasm, she could slow down, relax, breathe deeply, wait a moment or so and then let the tension build again. Experiment with this (either with your partner or while masturbating) to discover how long you have to stop–start, stop–start to get the most explosive orgasms. When you do allow yourself to come, clenching buttocks and inner thighs, deep breathing and pressing down just above your pubic bone all increase blood flow, which keeps the sensation going.

Here's an idea for you... **Play a game where you oil each other and try to give your mate an orgasm with a different part of your body from usual. (Boob job, anyone?)**

## NOT JUST FOR THE GIRLS

Advocates of all ways Eastern recommend 'injaculation', a way that men can experience multiple orgasms by 'coming' without ejaculation. This means he can go again right away, experience multiple bliss and, of course, keep going longer.

Try another idea... **Combine this with what you read in IDEA 45, Pressure – it's not a dirty word.**

How to do it? Business as usual until just before the point of 'no return'. Then swiftly, either you or your partner applies circular (quite heavy) pressure to your perineum, the space midway between your anus and the root of your penis. This causes pressure on the urethra and will stop you ejaculating, although you should still experience a deeply pleasurable, not to say mind-boggling, sensation. And you should still be hard – ready to play again should the mood take you. And it will, of course.

Some men love this. Some don't. One who doesn't is Grant Stoddard, who is quoted in *The Big Bang* by Em & Lo: 'The build up to the orgasm was momentarily more intense than usual. I realised I could go straight away again and did until I got bored and a bit depressed. The real shocker came when I went to the bathroom to find that my pee had more head on it than a pint of Guinness. In other words, I'd just come in my bladder. And that's fucked up.'

Defining idea... **'Made a hell of a discovery the other night. Eyelashes on the clit...can blink her off in no time.'**
DAN JENKINS, American writer

But worth a go.

**Q    What about women's multiple orgasms?**

A    *Theoretically, if a woman can come once, she can come multiple times. It's commonly believed that straight after a woman has come, she can't bear to have her clitoris touched. Sometimes true, but not always. Experiment with different techniques during masturbation. Swap to a different hand motion after you've come, or if you're using a vibrator try a different hot spot. Keep stimulation constant, but varied. Once you have the hang of that, masturbate to orgasm and stop masturbating completely after the first orgasm. Wait thirty seconds and then apply the same stimulation to the clitoris again. Shorten the waiting period until you can keep the stimulation at constant without it being uncomfortable, and experience orgasm after orgasm rolling over you.*

**Q    Is there any way we can practise peaking together?**

A    *You can go for the blended orgasm. This means applying stimulation at different pleasure points so excitement mounts. He can stimulate her G-spot, her clitoris and her perineum one after another in rotation. She can stimulate the head of his penis, the shaft and the prostate in rotation. This takes time, but should result in a long delayed and sweeter blend of intense pleasure and melting ecstasy when you come.*

How was it for you?

# 47

# Developing sexual mystique

**Yes, it's possible. Even if you've shared a bathroom for years.**

Last night I had a moment of despair. I walked by a pub where I overheard a man saying to his (male) companion, 'So go on then, have a guess. How many clear shots did Portugal have at goal?'

Admittedly even his mate looked bored, but I thought, 'Here I am, working at building more understanding between the sexes in my own small way. And it's a total waste of time. Men and women? Different species. What's the point?'

Then my natural Pollyanna spirit kicked in, 'Differences – you know what? They're a Good Thing. In fact, if you want to keep your love life hot, they're an Essential Thing. To carry on fancying your partner and to have them carrying on fancying you, you need a little distance between you, a little mystery, a little wildness in your soul.'

And if that doesn't come naturally, you need to work at it.

Here's an idea for you...

**In a nutshell, make it a habit that one night a week you do your own thing, no matter how busy you are. Remember, spending too much time inside together is terrible for your love life.**

'Male and female are different,' says relationship counsellor Paula Hall. 'And we've known since the sixties that if a couple want a stable relationship, it's worth working at maintaining that difference. It's what keeps the electric buzz between them.' She points out that studies by psychologists have already picked up on the dangers of becoming too alike. 'We call it "enmeshment" when couples become too similar,' says Hall. 'It's been known for a long time that it can have a detrimental impact on sexual desire.'

You probably think it's cosy that you share the same interests, friends, hopes, dreams, taste in soft furnishings. So it is. Congratulations. You're terrific mates. And carry on regardless if you want a great relationship without particularly exciting, or indeed plentiful, sex. However, if you want sex that makes your toes curl, you need a little separateness to keep desire alive.

You can be all things to a partner, but not to a lover. They cannot be all things to you.

There's an art to this. One woman I interviewed made a point of always being just a little bit cool with her husband every three or four months or so. 'Nothing serious,' she said, 'I'd just switch off from him a bit. Seem a little bit less easily pleased. A bit more interested in talking to my friends on the phone. Lock myself in the bathroom. Submerge myself in a book. Really trivial stuff. Worked like a charm. Within a week, he'd be suggesting weekends away in Paris and voluntarily arranging babysitting so we could go out to dinner.' (NB I can't resist the opportunity here to remind men of the huge aphrodisiac potential in occasionally arranging a babysitter. In most relationships, whether or not the woman works from home or not, she does the babysitting stuff – it's so goddamn nice when your partner sorts it out for once as it's such a clear signal that you want to spend some time with her. Try it.)

Read IDEA 22, *Sexual confidence*, for ideas on building self-esteem and individuality.

*Try another idea...*

All this withdrawing interest sounds suspiciously like game-playing – and you know what, it is! You can fake it a little bit like my interviewee, but it doesn't always work. What does always work is if both partners do it for real – keep interested in life, stay full of vim and brio for other projects, remain engaged with people outside of their relationship and be passionate about the world. Then, and here is the important bit, they bring that energy home and translate it into passion for each other. They do that by talking about their lives with such enthusiasm that their partners can't help get a kick out of their enthusiasm, charm, intelligence and all-round top-quality personality.

'An absence, the declining of an invitation to dinner, an unintentional, unconscious harshness are of more service than all the cosmetics and fine clothes in the world.'
MARCEL PROUST

*Defining idea...*

## THE LEAST YOU NEED TO DO...

Relationship psychologist Susan Quilliam points out that there are straightforward ways of making sure your relationship doesn't sink into the mire of 'enmeshment'.

**Rule 1.** All couples fall into a pattern of doing the same thing and being scared to suggest anything new because 'we don't do that'. But if you fancy doing something different, suggest it anyway. Don't argue if they say 'no'. The point has been made. You've reinforced in both your minds that you're different individuals.

**Rule 2.** Support your partner as much as possible when they're trying to be an individual. Don't dismiss new ideas and interests without thinking them through carefully.

**Rule 3.** Be yourself. Don't take on his or her interests and hobbies unless they genuinely interest you, too. We're equal but we're not the same.

**Q** **My partner's interest is hours spent in internet chatrooms. What's gone wrong?**

*How was it for you?*

**A** *You're insecure in your relationship for some reason and probably a very good reason. Whatever your partner chooses to do on their own that you view as a threat – chatrooms, lap dancing, drinking, Smurf collecting – isn't a problem in itself. It's the fact that you perceive it as a threat that's the problem. Yours is not a happy ship or your partner would stop or significantly cut down on the chatrooms when you expressed discomfort. A little bit of mystery only works to spice up healthy, functional relationships, and yours isn't. Time to start talking.*

**Q** **I tried being a bit withdrawn, but he didn't notice. Any ideas what I should try next?**

**A** *I'd guess that he's the one who proffers the cheek to be kissed and you're the one always doing the kissing. It's tough for kissers because they're genuinely focused on their mates pretty much to the detriment of everything else and it's hard to fake indifference. He knows what you're trying to do and kind of likes it. He'll ignore you even more – sorry, but that's the nature of the push–pull, passive–aggressive relationship you've formed. Until now it's worked for you, but maybe you now want something different. The solution for you is the solution for all of us when we want to change our relationships. Stop thinking about his reactions, expect nothing different from him and concentrate on you. Reintroduce passion into your own life. You've gone beyond the stage of playing games. It's time to get real about your life. If he's the only thing that really gets your juices going, change that fast.*

## 48

# See things differently

**Give yourself a real eye-opener.**

*Explore voyeurism and exhibitionism and bring a completely new verboten edge to your love life.*

The following fantasy role-plays depend on our love of looking and our love of being watched. Use these as a starting point to begin exploring your own voyeuristic or exhibitionistic fantasies – nearly all of us are turned on by one, and usually both. If you'd like to strip, but are too shy, then the second 'Peeping Tom' fantasy is a good place to start. You can start dropping clothes without feeling self-conscious, as you're not doing it (ostensibly) for an audience.

**IMAGINE...**

Your partner comes home to find the house lit by candles. You lead them to the bathroom where there is a scented bath waiting. You undress, blindfold and wash them. You don't let them do anything for themselves. Then you lead them to the bedroom, also lit only by candles, where there's a huge mirror propped to give a

Here's an idea for you...

**It can be very erotic to take turns ordering each other to perform. Some people love being ordered to strip or perform from the outset. Others hate it and bristle when their partner tells them what to do, even if it's done in an encouraging way. So be sensitive, as for one or both of you it may have to be a natural development.**

great reflection of the bed or, if that's not possible, the floor covered in cushions and quilts. Remove the blindfold and then make love, staring at yourself in the mirror, holding your lover's gaze. Try half closing your eyes so that you can fantasise that it isn't you, but another couple writhing inches away from you – accomplices at an orgy. Go one step further and imagine that the couple in the mirror are another couple that you're observing – to help the illusion, wear corsets, wigs, a new pair of heels, etc.

**IMAGINE...**

In the morning, you give your partner explicit written instructions of what you want them to do and at what hour you want them to start. At ten minutes before the appointed hour, you go to your bedroom, move clothes out of your wardrobe into the spare room, place a chair in the wardrobe and sit inside it with the door open a crack so you can see the bed. Your partner arrives in the bedroom. He or she follows the instructions you gave them earlier. They slowly begin to get ready for bed. If they get into it, this can be a long tease. They pass in and out of your field of vision, shedding clothes, trying on different clothes, lingerie or nightwear, examining their reflection, massaging in oils and creams before bed, phoning a friend and idly touching themselves as they talk, wandering out of the room to get themselves a drink. They are seemingly oblivious to your presence. Eventually they take up the position that you've stipulated and still 'unaware' that you're there, they give serious attention to bringing themselves off in front of your eager gaze.

## IMAGINE...

You are the stars of a live porn show. You've a clearly defined stage area (either your bed or a rug on your living room floor, brightly lit with spotlights). You both dress and prepare yourselves in your 'dressing room'. You can hear the pounding music in the background that you'll perform to and (imagine) the applause and excitement emanating from the audience. You take up position on your stage and begin to strip each other. Remember, everyone in the club has to see every detail and every act is exaggerated to give a maximum eyeful to the people standing, craning at the back. Massage oil into each other's bodies. When you start to have sex, remember this – it's a show. Everything has to be seen. Your audience loves it, and you can feel the tense silence as they watch you strip and the growing excitement as the sex becomes more explicit, more frenzied. You two get more excited, louder, more vocal, urging each other on verbally. When he comes, it should be over her body – the so-called 'money shot' beloved of porn films.

Turn to IDEA 23, *What you see...*, for more on visual arousal.

*Try another idea...*

'*There are only two guidelines for good sex, "don't do anything you don't really enjoy" and "find out your partner's needs and don't balk at them if you can help it".*'
DR ALEX COMFORT, author of *The Joy of Sex*

*Defining idea...*

211

How was it for you?

**Q** **Does all this have to be so complicated?**

A    It doesn't have to be. Park your car in a remote spot and play at being teenagers again. Taking risks in public is something that tends to diminish when we've been together for a while, which is a shame because although these risks may be uncomfortable, they'll make you feel far more daring than when you genuinely were a teenager. OK, you're respectable pillars of the community now, but you can still do it somewhere where you could be overlooked without taking much of a risk of it actually happening. Just thinking that you're being watched is a great turn-on.

**Q** **We want to film ourselves having sex. Where do we begin?**

A    If one of you is shy, play around with the last fantasy role-play in this idea. It's only one step away from setting up your camcorder while pretending to be porn stars. You'll want the lights on – fumbling in the dark feels good, but looks rubbish (which is why the above fantasy is a good starter because the spotlit 'stage' gets you used to performing in bright lights). You want the tripod fixed.

# 49

# Dealing with burnout

**That's what we call it when you don't want sex and you just don't care. In fact, you don't seem to care about anything much at all.**

*How do you know when you're dealing with burnout?*

**PROBLEM: TOO MANY PEOPLE WANT A BIT OF YOU**

**Solution: set boundaries and cut down on commitments**

People who don't set boundaries often end up playing out their frustrations in the bedroom: 'You don't give me what I need, so you won't get what you need.' This is equally true for the woman who withdraws sex as the man who, although he wants sex, isn't affectionate because he feels overburdened with responsibility. When you're too tired for sex or to give your partner what they need to feel good, the answer is to spend time cutting loose from all commitment. Time alone gives you a sense of balance and renewal, which can give you more energy.

How do you find that time? By setting boundaries. Here's what Dr Alan Altman says in his book *Making Love the Way We Used To, or Better*: 'You need to genuinely believe the following: You have needs. Those needs are as important as other people's needs. You can help others, but you do not have to be everyone's answer to everything. Sometimes saying no is a gift to the other person, who grows and becomes stronger by learning more self-reliance.'

Read books that thrilled you in your teens. Read books that make you horny. Listen to music that makes you feel sexual (or free, romantic, wild, independent). It could be Bruce Springsteen, Van Morrison or Morrissey (though if this is you, your sex life is likely to be the least of your problems). Whatever, if it rocks your boat then play it loud and play it often. Dance around your bedroom.

## PROBLEM: YOU'RE BORED WITH LIFE

### Solution: rediscover your passion and revel in pleasure

My definition of a mid-life crisis is pretty loose. It goes like this. You're aged anything from thirty-two upwards and you suddenly start feeling terribly, terribly scared. You're scared you've made mistakes. You're scared you haven't made enough mistakes. You're scared you'll be driving a Mondeo for the rest of your life. You're scared of your belly, more specifically the rate at which it's growing. These all amount to the same thing. You're scared of death.

Understandably, fear of death translates into a dissatisfaction with your version of the most life-affirming activity we've got – sex. And, more specifically, the partner you've chosen to have sex with. I'm not just talking about men here. What's fuelling the Viagra explosion is a whole raft of fifty-something women who are waking up and going, 'You know what, I'm bored of faking orgasms. Call this a sex life? I don't.' This is frightening the bejesus out of fifty-something men and they're hoping Viagra is the answer.

Anyway, I digress. The point is, if you're bored with having sex with your partner but you still love them, you have to talk instead of repeatedly saying 'no'. Tell your partner honestly, 'I'm worried. I'm rather fed up with

IDEA 44, *It's not all in your mind*, **has more on the physical and mental obstacles to a great sex life.**

*Try another idea...*

everything. I don't have juice for anything much, and with your help I want to get back my va-va-voom.' Then you can negotiate more time for yourself, more holidays together, the purchase of a nice big vibrator, dressing up as Santa Claus. Whatever it takes to get more pleasure into your life, because pleasure is the only cure for a mid-life crisis and all other forms of burnout. Your partner might not like some of your ideas – they're never going to think that a Harley Davidson is a great idea and they're certainly not going to warm to the leather chaps. But if yours is a good healthy relationship then they'll live with whatever it takes to return you to the happy love bunny you were of yore. Unless, of course, it threatens them or the relationship, in which case you don't have a healthy relationship and you need the sort of help that's outside the scope of this idea. Good luck with the therapy.

*'Sex without love is an empty experience, but, as empty experiences go, it's one of the best.'*
WOODY ALLEN

*Defining idea...*

215

*How was it for you?*

**Q    I hate my job. I'm exhausted, but there's no way I can cut down on my workload. What can I do?**

A    *It's impossible to get in touch with our inner sex god or goddess if you're totally stressed out and exhausted. David Deida says that working too hard can be detrimental to some relationships, especially for women, and that 'common financial needs have replaced commitment and desire as the motivating forces in many relationships'. I want to disagree with him, especially about the emphasis on women. But I can't. Everywhere I see many women and some men who are knackered and confused. Who can argue with the fact that 'common financial needs' have hijacked many couples' lives, including yours? Lack of interest in sex is only one of your problems. Anger, resentment and disappointment are all probably waving their hands to be noticed, too. But unless you're on absolute subsistence, then you have choices. You're going to have to have constructive, creative discussions with your partner about exactly what you need to get happy and stay that way.*

**Q    Exactly what do you mean by getting more pleasure into my life? If I knew how, I would.**

A    *The surest route to pleasure and passion is to get creative. Make a habit or expressing what you really think and feel. There are a million ways to do this – organising a pub quiz can be creative if you want it to be. I can't tell you what makes you passionate or gives you pleasure. Some spiritual types would say that's what we're on the planet to discover. You either pursue your potential for creativity, passion and pleasure or you don't. It's your call.*

# Dream time

**Sexual fantasy – a short cut to great sex.**

*Read on if your response was, 'Who's got the time?'*

Somebody once said that sexual fantasy was the 'thinking man's television', and they weren't kidding. Hours of entertainment and you don't even have to leave your sofa to enjoy it. If you get up off your butt and take your fantasies into the bedroom, they'll give you explosive orgasms, too. What goes on in your mind is as important as what's going on around your genitals. However, just like talking dirty, it has to be your own 'script'. Many people read the lists of top male fantasies or top female fantasies (usually both headed by lesbian sex) and think 'bollocks'. I'm not being judgemental. If you're a woman who thinks about two birds getting stuck in and this drives you over the edge, terrific. But if it doesn't, you shouldn't give up finding out what does. Men tend to have more access to porn, and that hotwires their fantasies and preferences pretty early on. Women don't usually have this advantage and by the time they get to adulthood are often too busy unloading the dishwasher to give a toss. But bear with me. Even if sexual fantasy isn't a big bit of your life right now, it's a habit well worth getting into.

## WHY?

Sexual fantasy increases your libido. The more you think about sex, the more you want it. Plus, just a glimmer of the thought of your fantasy during sex will increase your pleasure a hundred-fold and if you're a woman it'll make orgasm faster (if

Here's an idea for you... **Once you've discovered fantasyland, up the dirtiness quotient. The true power of fantasy lies in forbidden thoughts, so try thinking of some real extremes. Remember, this has nothing to do with who you are in real life.**

you're a bloke, more enjoyable). Also, a strong fantasy life is invaluable for those times when your partner reaches for you and you're not sure if you can be bothered. Letting your favourite fantasy tickle your imagination for a second or two can be the deciding factor as to whether you respond with alacrity or shrug them off. My view is that happier relationships result when the response is the former.

*Defining idea...* *'I caused my husband's heart attack. In the middle of lovemaking, I took the paper bag off my head. He dropped the Polaroid and keeled over and so did the hooker. It would have taken me half an hour to untie myself and call the paramedics, but fortunately the Great Dane could dial.'*
JOAN RIVERS

**WHAT?**

A friend once recounted some of her dreams to me, 'I fantasise about having two men at one time or having sex with someone else while my boyfriend watches. I fantasise about getting oral sex from under the table at a restaurant or about being screwed during a gynaecological exam. Usually I don't have time to make an elaborate fantasy during sex, but conjuring up any one of these quick images will do.'

Your fantasy might be something that you won't find on a list of 'top fantasies'. For instance, there's some evidence that in the post-feminist age, many women love the idea of homosexual sex – but with men not women. A gay man means a good body and a challenge – just the sort of thing a feisty woman would enjoy fantasising about. (Hmm...perhaps that's Madonna's thing.) But women willing to admit to it are rare. Hell, women even realising that thinking about gay men could do it for them are rare. As with most things to do with sex, gender politics probably come into it. Women aren't sexually liberated enough to talk about a fantasy that doesn't turn straight men on. In

**For inspiration look to IDEA 51, *Fantasy destinations.***

*Try another idea...*

fact, since erect dicks are in the equation, it'll probably threaten them. This could be one reason why women don't fantasise as much – their fantasies don't appear on any of those lists so they think they're weird and give up on them. If none of the traditional female fantasies ring your bell, then read *My Secret Garden*, *Women on Top* or *Men in Love* by Nancy Friday – an absolute eye-opener (and a turn-on) for both sexes.

## HOW?

You can either be in the fantasy, or observe your fantasy as you would a film. Start telling yourself a story. A story where you're the hero/heroine – as gorgeous as you like. An American comic had a great gag, 'When I fantasise, I'm someone else.' And although it's meant to be funny, he's got it in one: you can be the person you'd like to be.

Your fantasy can be filled with people you know really well or people you glimpsed on a bus twenty years ago, and again they can be idealised versions – more exciting, demanding, inventive. Think in detail. Tell yourself these stories while masturbating. Imagine hands grasping, tongues licking, words being whispered. (You don't need the whole story when you're making love, just a flash of detailed scene.) It takes practice.

*Defining idea...*

'I say to men, "OK, pretend you're a burglar and you break in and throw me down on the bed and make me suck your cock." And they're horrified. "No, no, it would degrade you." Exactly. Degrade me when I ask you to.'
LISA PALAC, American writer

219

**Q    Fantasies – no problem – but they're very raunchy. Should I
    share them?**

*A    Couples are always being exhorted to share fantasies, and this can be a big
    mistake. Men know this. I always remember the shock of asking the most
    conventional boyfriend I ever had to tell me what he fantasised about and
    he blithely and immediately answered 'golden showers'. I was stunned into
    silence. Later, intrigued, I asked him more. Either my boyfriend was having
    me on or didn't want to ever go there in reality (me too, if I'm being
    honest) as he clammed up. Some sharing will definitely enhance your
    lovemaking, but maybe it would be better to keep the one about defecating
    nuns to yourself.*

**Q    Can you give me some inspiration?**

*A    Both sexes fantasise about sex with a stranger. Women get off on the
    element of being forced – to strip, to have sex with one or multiple men.
    Often these fantasies get exotic – the sultan and the harem, the plundering
    pirate. Another version is the casting couch or the job interview where you
    have to give sex to get on in your career. Showing off is big for women –
    stripping or lap dancing – and the 'seducing a virgin' works for both sexes.
    Women often imagine having to teach one or many young men how to
    'pleasure' a woman. And, of course, there's lesbian sex and being watched
    secretly. Another big favourite is sex with someone forbidden – your
    partner's best friend rather than your mother-in-law, obviously. Or maybe
    not... There I go, being judgemental.*

dream

# 51

# Fantasy destinations

**Great places to have sex – and you don't have to get a babysitter.**

Doing it differently is part of the foundations for constantly exciting sex. Every so often, make one of your dates an at-home soiree. Decide on your fantasy destination — use your imagination and introduce as much role-play as you feel comfortable with.

A fantasy destination is a good laugh. It's a cheap game and it gets your creative juices flowing. How many classic/cliched love scenes can you re-enact without leaving your house? Here are some to get you going:

## TOP FIVE FANTASY DESTINATIONS

### The alpen lodge in a blizzard (your living room)
It's winter. Deep winter. You are two climbers who've had to take shelter in a remote log cabin, cut off from the rest of the human race and locked fast by a

Here's an idea for you... **Plan your fantasy trip carefully. Take time to run through the scenario in your mind and write your own script (mentally). Unless you're both brilliant at improvisation and have a bit of a competitive streak, then it will typically take two or three fantasy destinations for you to get a grip on it.**

blizzard. You've no electricity, little food but luckily lots of brandy. You spread a blanket in front of the log fire, light a couple of candles and sip at your brandy. Outside the wind is howling. Your fellow climber is looking more attractive by the minute. Soon it seems a very good idea to get under the blanket (or better still, into a very cosy sleeping bag) and huddle together for warmth...

**Working late at the office (your kitchen)**
One of you is the boss. The boss has very high standards and expects a great deal from their assistant. The assistant is working late one night (at your kitchen table posing as a desk), bent over their work with only a desk lamp for illumination. Suddenly, the boss strides in and throws a sheaf of papers at the hapless assistant's head and lets loose with a stream of invective along the lines of, 'This is rubbish. If you want to keep your job, you're going to have to be punished until you do it better.' The hapless assistant is tied up to a chair while the boss begins to undress the assistant and themselves and hisses, 'You'd like to touch me, but you're so incompetent you wouldn't know what to do with it.' The boss then proceeds to show the assistant how it should be done, ordering the assistant to help make amends for past mistakes.

**The sauna (your bathroom)**
It's very hot and steamy (thanks to your shower being on full). So steamy that at first you don't see that someone else is sharing the sauna with you. Then you notice a figure sitting close by wrapped in a white towel. You smile uncertainly then shut

your eyes and relax, letting the steam overwhelm you. You open your eyes. Your companion is staring at you. Their towel falls open. Everyone is supposed to wear swimsuits but you never do, and they obviously don't either. You're embarrassed. Should you point out that their towel has slipped or let your own slip a little too…?

**Still not convinced? For some inspiration read IDEA 14, *Surprise!***

*Try another idea…*

## The camping holiday (your garden, in summer)

You and a friend have gone on a holiday – walking in the hills. After a long day, you set up camp (or settle under the stars in your sleeping bags) in the middle of nowhere. You switch on a torch, have some dinner, share some jokes, drink some wine, play a game of cards. Before you know it, the game of cards has turned into a strip version of the game and things get very friendly in your tent (or, if you're unperturbed by the neighbours, under the stars)…

## Murder in the dark (your house, with the lights off)

You're both guests at a country house party. A fellow guest has suggested a game of murder in the dark. One of you goes off to hide somewhere in the dark silent house. One of you is the murderer who stealthily hunts them down, getting closer and closer. But when the murderer finds the victim, there's another surprise for both of them…

*'The most romantic thing a woman ever said to me in bed was, "Are you sure you're not a cop?"'*
LARRY BROWN, American comedian

*Defining idea…*

**Q** **I'm game, but my partner thinks the whole thing is ridiculous. Any more tips?**

*A* *Pick one of the scenarios that involves minimal role-playing. Out of the above, that's the camping one. If they absolutely refuse to have sex in a tent in your back garden under cover of darkness, you may have to give up on this one. However, you can try talking about fantasy situations in the privacy of your own bed, as just talking fantasy can be a terrific fillip to your love life.*

**Q** **We tried the tent in the garden, but by the time we'd put it up it was hard to get in character. How do we stop the organising getting in the way?**

*A* *Admittedly, sorting it out together can be a bit off-putting. It's more fun if you take turns being the 'party co-ordinator' responsible for gathering the props, decorating the room if necessary, organising outfits if appropriate and making sure any food or alcohol that's required are on tap. Leave a note explaining the scenario, with any clothes you want your lover to wear laid out on the bed.*

# 52

# Are you sexually mature?

**It is big and it is clever.**

I've got a theory about what happens when couples are no longer connecting sexually. That theory goes something like this...

Men and women may enjoy casual sex in much the same way, but when it comes to the long haul – the big relationship where the expectations and desire of each partner is that it lasts for the foreseeable future – different attitudes towards what constitutes closeness can develop over the years. I'm going to generalise like crazy, so you two might not conform to this pattern, but on the whole women seem to show their love through emotional closeness and need their partner to show them that he loves them through emotional closeness – talking, discussion, showing empathy (that means picking your socks up off the bedroom floor in case you were wondering). However, men, on the whole, show their love through physically doing something – earning money, cleaning the car, sexual contact. Sex, not discussion, is their way of showing love and feeling loved.

Men don't place enough value on emotional contact, and women don't place enough value on physical contact. That's fine when things are going well, as both partners 'put out' for each other. But if a change happens in their lifestyle and one partner withdraws the contact the other needs, they get caught up in a vicious cycle. He isn't encouraged to extend emotional closeness to her while she's

Here's an idea for you...

**Remember the old saying about walking in another's shoes if you want to understand them? When your partner has upset or irritated you, make a real effort to understand why they behaved in that way. Still confused? Make them explain what's going through their head. Silence is the worst thing you can do.**

withdrawing physical contact from him, and she in turn can't understand how he can expect her to have sex when they're barely grunting at each other and he spends entire evenings watching TV. Their sex life at best is mediocre, sporadic and unsatisfying. And it stays that way.

This is the pattern of the sexually immature couple. They might have shagged like stoats in their youth. They may have more sexual experience than Peter Stringfellow and Jordan combined. But sexual experience has nothing to do with sexual maturity.

## SIGNS OF SEXUAL MATURITY

### You don't wait for sex to just happen

You make sex a priority. You go to work when you're tired. You call your mother when you're stressed. You feed the kids when you have a headache. Sexually mature couples give sex the same priority they give other important things in their lives. They at least remain open to the idea of having sex at any time. They trust that their lover will find a way to turn them on.

### You know the importance of doing it differently

Not least because your relationship, your body and your life won't stay the same. Being prepared to change the way you have sex prepares you for the inevitable changes that will occur in your life. It's something that brings you respite when life gets messy, joy when life gets dreary, and comfort when illness or death leave their scars on your psyche. Sex with your loving partner is where you go when you want to celebrate life's happiness, and it's where you run to hide from life's hurts.

Turn to IDEA 39, *Let a woman be a woman and a man be a man*, for ideas on finding new ways to relate to each other.

*Try another idea...*

## You use sex as a way to show your partner that they're loved

Reaching out to your partner helps you avoid passive–aggressive games. You don't let just one person always initiate sex because that means the other has the power to refuse or withdraw. Sex can become a punishment or reward and if this is your relationship, that's a dangerous place to be, because both of you will end up hostile or resenting each other for different reasons.

## You actively think of how you can use your sexuality to make your partner happier

This isn't just about giving your partner orgasms. Sex is a gift. You sometimes do stuff for no reward. Lots of people find it really difficult to make a gift of themselves. Even when they push themselves to sexual extremes in an effort to keep the spark between them alive, their relationship isn't intimate enough to maintain all the emotional intensity that scary sex throws up.

## You try for each other

And by reading ideas like this you let the other person know it. Continually being prepared to come out to bat for your relationship is as loving as it gets. Congratulations.

*'The highest level of sexual excitement is in a monogamous relationship.'*
WARREN BEATTY, a man who should know

*Defining idea...*

*How was it for you?*

**Q** **The stuff about being intimate hit home. I feel that we're at our most awkward in bed. What should we do?**

*A* *This is really common. Was it always this way or did it happen after a big life change like having a baby? Sensate focus was invented for couples like you. Try in small ways to break down the barriers to intimacy and if you can't, couple counselling can help.*

**Q** **I get so angry with my partner. He puts little into our relationship and still expects sex. How can I deal with my resentment?**

*A* *Try having sex whenever he wants for a month. And initiate sex once a week. Break through your anger and hostility – and don't think I'm blaming you for being angry, it's just not getting you anywhere. Show compassion. Show willing. And if he's still expecting and not giving, insist that he spend half an hour talking to you every day. And if he won't do this, phone Relate.*

# The end...

Or is it a new beginning? We hope that the ideas in this book will have inspired you to try some new things to spice up your sex life and encouraged you to think about it a little differently. You should be well on the way now to seeing how you can recapture the rapture.

So why not let us know about it? Tell us how you got on. What did it do for you – what helped you to light the blue touch paper again? Maybe you've got some tips of your own you want to share. If you liked this book you may find we have more brilliant ideas for other areas that could help change your life for the better.

You'll find the Infinite Ideas crew waiting for you online at www.infideas.com.

Or if you prefer to write, then send your letters to:
*Re-energise Your Sex Life*
The Infinite Ideas Company Ltd
Belsyre Court, 57 Woodstock Road, Oxford OX2 6JH, United Kingdom

We want to know what you think, because we're all working on making our lives better too. Give us your feedback and you could win a copy of another *52 Brilliant Ideas* book of your choice. Or maybe get a crack at writing your own.

Good luck. Be brilliant.

# Offer one

**CASH IN YOUR IDEAS**

We hope you enjoy this book. We hope it inspires, amuses, educates and entertains you. But we don't assume that you're a novice, or that this is the first book that you've bought on the subject. You've got ideas of your own. Maybe our author has missed an idea that you use successfully. If so, why not send it to info@infideas.com, and if we like it we'll post it on our bulletin board. Better still, if your idea makes it into print we'll send you £50 and you'll be fully credited so that everyone knows you've had another Brilliant Idea.

# Offer two

**HOW COULD YOU REFUSE?**

Amazing discounts on bulk quantities of Infinite Ideas books are available to corporations, professional associations and other organizations.

For details call us on:
+44 (0)1865 292045
fax: +44 (0)1865 292001
or e-mail: info@infideas.com

# Where it's at...

Agatston, Dr Arthur, 96

Allen, Woody, 215

Altman, Dr Alan, 51, 213

Alvarez, Julia, 3

anal sex, 89–93

antici...pa...tion, see delaying orgasm

anti-depressant effect of sex, 36

aphrodisiac, 22–23, 167, 169, 205

    see also danger

asking your partner to try something (we're not

    talking a new flavour of risotto here), 69

B&D, see bondage and discipline

bathroom, 3, 54, 66, 149–152, 200, 203–204, 209,

    224

    see also showerhead

baths, 55, 78

Beatty, Warren, 229

better orgasms, 27, 121–123

blow jobs, 103–106, 145–148

Blue, Violet, 90, 117, 118

bondage and discipline (B&D), 133–137

bored with sex, 1–4

    see also breathing, pulse, body still warm

breathing, 134, 148, 179–182, 199

Brown, Larry, 225

Bukowski, Charles, 101

bum, 70, 72, 91, 93, 118, 146

    see also butt plug

burnout, 155, 193, 213, 215

butt plug, 93, 165

Carey, Jaqueline, 134

CAT, see coital alignment technique

Chase, Chevy, 115

Cheever, John, 197

climate of confidence, 7

clit pump, 164

clitoral stimulation, 17–18, 20, 77–79, 126–127,

    130

clitoris, 17, 19–20, 41, 57, 78, 79, 100, 114, 117,

    119, 130, 139, 140–142, 148, 150, 151,

    159–160, 164, 198, 201

cock ring, 160

coital alignment technique (CAT), 17–20, 127

Coldwell, Liz, 43

Collins, J.K., 99, 100

Comfort, Dr Alex, 211

Corn, Laura, 59, 61

Cox, Tracey, 2, 7

cunnilingus, 117–120, 141

Dalai Lama, 83

danger as an aphrodisiac, 167–170

deep throat, 148

Deida, David, 171, 172, 182, 216

delaying orgasm, 199–201

depression, 192

dildos, 90–92, 124, 164–165

Diller, Phyllis, 155

dirty little secrets, 169, 183–186

doctor, seeing your, 191–194

doctors, fantasy role play, 82, 108

Dodson, Betty, 161

dogging, 69, 72

Dutton, Judy, 127


ejaculate, female, 42–43

Em and Lo, 27, 71, 105, 135

emotional contact, 227

exhibitionism, 209


fantasies, fantasy, 8–11, 27, 47–50, 66, 72, 79, 101, 106–109, 111, 116, 134, 164, 169, 198, 209, 212, 217, 218, 219, 223–224, 226

fantasy destinations, 219, 223–226

feedback (it's about talking, not Jimi Hendrix' guitar technique), 3, 26, 28, 92, 108, 116, 126, 139, 143, 196, 198, 232

feeling better about ourselves through sex, 37

fellatio, 7, 103, 147

    *see also* giving head, blow jobs

Fellini, Federico, 189

feminism, 172

fights, fighting, 38, 74, 86–87, 153–157

fisting, 69

five inches erect (that's 12.7 cm), 96

flirting, 49, 96, 111

foreplay, 33, 45, 61, 66, 76–77, 119–120, 175–176, 190

Freud, Sigmund 41, 173


getting your lover to do something differently, 5

giving head, 120, 139

    *see also* fellatio, blow jobs

going down, 104, 106, 117

    *see also* fellatio, cunnilingus, blow jobs, giving head

going out with each other, 14

golden shower, *see* peeing on your man

gone off sex, 11, 188, 191–194

Gray, John, 85, 86

Groening, Matt, 146

G-spot, 17, 41–45, 126, 131, 161, 201


Hall, Jerry, 185

hand job, 4, 113–116

Hite Report, 77, 100

Hite, Shere, 57

    *see also* Spoonerisms

Hooper, Ann, 9

Hopkins, Tom, 36

Hutchins, D. Claire, 78, 79


immune system, 38

initiating sex, 11, 74–75, 229–230


Jenkins, Dan, 200

Jong, Erica, 11


kaizen, 7, 61, 73–76, 131, 145

Kegel, Dr Arnold, 121

Kegels, 121–124

kinky, 3, 56, 67, 69–72, 91, 135, 185

Lapides, Beth, 67

Lawrence, D. H., 177

libido, 2, 9, 33, 81, 83, 96, 101, 169, 182, 189,
191–194, 217

Lightwoman, Leonora, 181

Litvinoff, Sarah, 11

long-term partner, 51, 95

long-term, relationships, 35, 39, 42, 51–53, 82, 88,
95, 101

losing weight, 98

love but no lust, 53

love quotient (LQ), 85–88

LQ, *see* love quotient

lubricate, lubrication, lube, 91–92, 100, 114, 119,
163

lust, 10, 26, 33, 52–53, 57, 89, 187–189, 194


making a date for sex, 33

massage, massaging 1, 3, 56–58, 63, 67, 74, 80,
92, 98, 174, 181, 195–198, 210

Masterton, Graham, 43

masturbating, 17, 80, 113, 115, 124, 126, 128, 146,
161, 187, 199, 201, 219

McConville, Brigid, 25, 52

McGraw, Dr Phil, 97

meditation, 2, 180

Mickins, Beverly, 23

missionary, 19, 20, 78, 126, 130, 132
*see also* positions

Monroe, Marilyn, 57–58

mood for sex, in the, 149, 189

multiple orgasms, 122, 200–201

nipples, 56, 146, 184

O'Rourke, P.J., 104, 109, 165

oral sex, 8, 17, 62, 91, 103–106, 116, 117–120,
139–143, 145, 184, 198, 218

orgasms, 3–4, 17–18, 20, 22, 25, 27, 38, 41–42,
58, 78–80, 84, 91–93, 113–128, 131, 135–136,
141–142, 146–147, 150–151, 165, 175, 179,
187, 199–201, 214, 217, 229
faster orgasms for women, 125–128
simultaneous, 18, 20, 125, 126
women coming as easily as men, 77

Palac, Lisa, 219

partner(s), 2, 4, 6, 10–15, 19, 22, 24–25, 28–31,
33, 39, 44, 51–53, 57–59, 61, 68–69, 72,
74–75, 78–83, 85–88, 92, 95–96, 98, 104, 106,
113–114, 116–117, 120, 126, 128, 131–135,
139, 145, 150, 153, 154, 157, 160, 162, 165,
167, 170, 173, 174, 176–177, 179, 181,
183–184, 187–190, 194, 196–197, 199–200,
203–207, 209–210, 213–216, 218, 226–230

passion for life, 53–54

PC, *see* pubococcygeal muscles
*see also* Kegels

peeing on your man, 137

penetrative sex, 1, 2, 17, 42, 77, 83, 188

penis, 18–19, 23, 43–44, 77, 92, 96–97, 100,
103–105, 115–116, 126, 131, 140, 142,
146–148, 159–160, 164, 184, 191, 198,
200–201
size, *see* five inches erect

perineum, 93, 104, 114, 140, 146-147, 159, 200-201
physical intimacy, 14, 83
porn, 10, 18, 27, 43, 91, 99, 102, 119, 131, 148, 166-167, 176, 185, 211, 212, 217
positions, 19, 44, 74, 114, 119, 127, 129, 131-132, 147, 181
praise, 6, 8, 26
prioritising your relationship, 13
prostate, 91-92, 146, 164-165, 201
prostitution fantasies, 47
Proust, Marcel, 205
pubococcygeal muscles (PC), 78, 121-126, 165

Quayle, Marilyn, 53
quickie, 21-24, 100, 185, 190
Quilliam, Susan, 206

recharging your sexual batteries, 65
rediscovering your passion, 214
Rivers, Joan, 19, 218
role-play, 117, 132, 134, 137, 164, 212, 223
romance novels, 10
Roosevelt, Eleanor, 131
Rowland, Helen, 123
Rudner, Rita, 151
rule of difference, 74

S&M, see sadism and masochism
sadism and masochism (S&M), 133
saying 'no', 187-190
sensate focus, 1-4

sensuality, 1, 4, 55, 177
sex as a means to defuse stress, 36
sex drives out of sync, 4, 81-84
sex on the brain, 9
sex the focus of your break, 65
sex toys, 93, 160-161
sex, initiating, 11, 74-75, 229-230
sex, not fancying, 33, 35
sex, not having the energy for, 29
sexual confidence, 95-97
sexual desert, 188, 190
sexual fantasy, see fantasies
sexual mystique, 53, 203-207
sexual secrets, 183-186
sexually mature, 173, 227-230
Shandling, Gary, 193
shared memories, 14, 16, 66, 183
shower, golden, see golden shower
showerhead, 151-152
showering, 2, 55-58, 62, 67, 90, 128, 150-152, 196, 224
simultaneous orgasm, 18, 20, 125, 126
sixty-nine (69), 131
    see also positions
sleep is the new sex, 14, 29-33
slut sex, 47-50
South Beach Diet, 96
spanking, 137
St Claire, Olivia, 179
strap-ons, 164
stress, 38, 121
stress, using sex to defuse, 36

surprise factor, 59
surprising your lover, 60
synchronicity, 83, 128

taking a break from sex, 1, 147
talking dirty, 25–28, 217
Tantric, 113, 175–178, 180–181
Taschen, Benedikt, 180
thrusting, 18–19, 43, 78, 132, 139, 148
tiredness, 29, 30
Tisdale, Sally, 91
toys, 93, 111, 150, 159–162

Ustinov, Peter, 87

vaginal muscles, 78
Viagra, 194, 214
vibrators, 44–45, 77, 84, 90, 93, 100, 104, 126, 128, 131, 147, 152, 159, 160–162, 165, 201, 215
visual stimulation, 99, 101
voyeurism, 209

Wax, Ruby, 169
why sex goes off the boil, 171–174
Williamson, Marianne, 140
woman on top, 131
    *see also* positions
women coming as easily as men, 77

yoga, yogic 174, 180

# Even more brilliant ideas...

## Re-energise your relationship
Dr Sabina Dosani & Peter Cross

"How can you recapture those golden moments when your relationship was new and exciting, when the thought of just speaking to your lover made your heart pound?"

"Would you both now rather watch the TV than talk, cuddle or even kiss? And as for sex - is that now reserved for public holidays in leap years? Well, it doesn't need to be like that! With a little effort, and using our practical and inspiring ideas, you can light that fire again!"
**– Dr Sabina Dosani and Peter Cross**

## Look gorgeous always
Linda Bird

"Looking beautiful is about much more than possessing fantastic cheek-bones and endless legs, though of course, great genes do help. The good news is that vitality, confidence, a savvy wardrobe, a few great make up and grooming tricks can work wonders too."

"The trick is to look after yourself, and to learn how to use what you've got to your best advantage. It's about maximising your beautiful bits, minimising the less beautiful ones, and faking a few more. "

"Look gorgeous always will help you unlock the ravishing creature that lies within. It provides lots of simple but ingenious tips that that I've learned from the leading lights in health and beauty. Try these brilliant ideas today – and feel more gorgeous, instantly!" – **Linda Bird**

## Raise pre-teens

Dr Sabina Dosani and Peter Cross

*"We all know we can do a better job of bringing up our children. We're not super-parents ourselves, but we are experts in parenting and child psychology with long experience of the sort of problems families can face. Raising children is one of the most important and rewarding things you can do in life. It can be challenging, even maddening, but if you get it right it is one of life's great experiences. If you are looking for some brilliant ideas for doing it better, this book's for you. Our ideas will help you and your children get more out of family life and help your children enjoy their own lives more."* – **Dr Sabina Dosani** and **Peter Cross**

## Whole health

Kate Cook

*"The media seem to be obsessed with the deterioration of our physical and mental health. All you hear about is obesity, disease, binge drinking and drug addiction. And what's the usual answer?"*

*"Some complex detoxification programme, diets that mean you can only eat raw pulses and exercise regimes that will train you to be a marathon runner. Oh yes, and counselling so that your parents can ultimately take the blame for your problems."*

*"Here's a different approach that I've used myself and with friends and clients. It does involve exercise and diet but above all else – common sense! The net result will be a happier, healthier you."*
**Kate Cook**